WALLEYE
FISHING
TODAY

by
Tom Zenanko

Artwork by Buzz Buczynski, Brookston, Minn.
Editorial thanks to Pat Dolan, Minneapolis
Cover and Inside Photos by Author

Tom Zenanko Outdoors

Library of Congress No. 82-24146
ISBN 0-9610296-09

Printed by
Nystrom Publishing Inc.
Maple Grove, Minnesota

WALLEYE FISHING TODAY

TABLE OF CONTENTS

This book is dedicated to all my good friends who freely gave of their time and experience to help me along in my chosen career; To my loyal family whose constant support kept me pushing ahead; and to the people who haven't yet had the thrill of catching their first walleye.

Introduction

It was a crowded room with people standing along the back row for the last two hours. I had just announced there would be time for only one more question. A dozen hands went up and I selected an older gray haired gentleman who spoke with a loud deep voice.

"I've recently retired and plan on doing a lot of walleye fishing this summer. My question, Tom, is that your seminar was the only one I have been to where I actually understood the terms and logic you used to catch walleyes. Every magazine that claims to be for fishermen has to have a glossary to describe the fancy words and terms that they consider you HAVE TO know to be a good fisherman. Is there a book that walks you through the things you REALLY need to know about walleye fishing?"

This gentleman had a problem all right, because at that time there was not a single walleye book on the market written for the average person with up-to-date information about the new trends and equipment that really play a helpful role in your fishing success.

Walleye Fishing Today fits its title perfectly because the recent improvements in tackle, boats and electronic gadgets need to be put into perspective so that the consumers know how these new advances can be used most productively.

Everywhere anglers look for information from the "experts," they are surrounded by sales pitches and gimmicks along with a pile of fancy terms I think are dreamed up just to sound impressive. The most recent figures say that 20% of the fishermen catch 80% of the fish! This book is here to help that 80% better understand walleyes and to show the true "bread and butter" methods that DO catch fish!

The more fishermen get into fishing, the more they realize just how important "the little things" can be to their success. In that way this book also fits the needs of that upper 20% where fishing might seem to be getting too complicated and gets right down to the bare facts.

I never saw that older gray haired gentleman again nor learned his name, but he planted the seed for this book. It has become my firm belief that a good fishing book or magazine can be done well by using plain English so that everyone can be more successful and better enjoy the truly great sport of fishing.

The Way of the Walleye

If you plan on catching more walleyes after reading this book, it is important to start fishing by having a better understanding of the fish itself. The old expression "you need to think like a fish," isn't that far off.

Although many anglers across the country consider walleyes the only fish that swims, others would compare its fighting ability to that of an old shoe.

The range of ol' marble eyes extends as far north as the Arctic Circle and as far south as Louisiana. As the popularity of this noble fish expands, so does its range. The eastern and western seaboard states that did not have a natural walleye population now have a very successful stocking programs to introduce this fish to many of the newer reservoirs, which are often perfect habitat for the walleye.

As you travel around this continent of ours, you may run into some strangely named fish such as white salmon, glasseye, pickerel, gum pike or walleye pike. These are all commonly found nicknames given to the walleye. The common reference to "pike" is a misnomer; actually the walleye is a member of the perch family. Its name comes from its glowing eyes that give the impression they are blinded or "wall-eyed."

The world record walleye came from Old Hickory Lake, Tennessee in 1960 and weighed 25 pounds. This beauty was 41 inches long and had a girth of 29 inches. For a walleye to grow this large, three things had to be available: adequate food, almost perfect water temperatures for a longer annual growth rate, and a lack of competition with other walleyes. This, along with a lot of luck, will give a walleye a long and prosperous life.

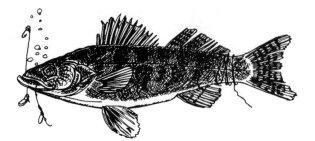

The next world record walleye (stizostedion vitreum vitreum)

In my conversations with Minnesota biologists, we often talked about how walleyes defeat the odds of nature to live naturally and reproduce in our lakes and rivers.

According to Bill Johnson, area fisheries manager in the Grand Rapids area of Minnesota, "With all the things that could turn against a spawning walleye, it's surprising that ANY walleyes exist in our lakes."

Let's take a look at the life cycle of a walleye so you can better understand how tough it really is to be a walleye.

Female walleyes reach maturity in about four to seven years, depending on the water temperature of the lake or river they come from. The warmer the water, the faster the growth cycle. In northern parts of Minnesota a seven year old female walleye will weigh only two and a half pounds! That same fish in

For walleyes to grow from an egg to these sizes, the odds are often a million to one!

Arkansas could be five pounds or more.

Male walleyes reach maturity in a shorter time, usually three to five years of age, but are the smaller of the two when compared with females of the same age class.

Walleyes begin to show signs of spawning interest when water temperatures are only 34 degrees. Since spawning females have been known to travel 200 miles to reach their spawning sites, some researchers believe they possess a homing instinct like a salmon, although not nearly as intense. With this need to travel such great distances to spawn, do they return to their original home when spawning is completed? As with much of the research that has been done on walleyes, no definite answers have been found. There is a strong belief that walleyes do indeed have home grounds and migrate to reach spawning areas only to return to the same summering areas year after year.

When the water temperatures reach 42 to 52 degrees, walleyes seek out areas of gravel to small rock in waters of less than three feet to spawn. The key ingredient to a good spawning site is current flow or wave action. Small rivers are often ideal spawning sites, but in many lakes a shallow windswept point or shoreline can offer enough wave action to meet the needs of the spawning walleye. Of course not all areas where walleyes exist have perfect textbook spawning sites. Often bridge pilings can serve as a kind of man-made spawning site. It is not that unusual to find a shallow reef in the middle of a lake teeming with spawning walleye. The presence of gravel or small rocks and a constant flow of fresh water around the eggs, however, are essential factors for successful reproduction.

Spawning activity occurs at night in three feet of water or less, and studies show that most females discharge their eggs in one evening. This is not to say that all the fish in a given body of water spawn the same night. Each female walleye will tend to ripen at her own rate. In a normal spring it is very possible to have walleye spawning over a two week period.

The male walleye is the first to enter the spawning grounds and the last to leave. In the actual egg laying process, the ratio is often four males to one female. Literally hundreds of male walleye will roam the shallows of a lake looking for females. Even after a male has spawned with one female, he will continue to search for more females and will even travel from one spawning area to another in his quest to find ripe females.

The average female lays about 30,000 eggs and in a natural setting you can expect that approximately 5% of the eggs will hatch into fry in about 20 days. It will take about 125 thousand fry to make a pound! At this point, future fishing success is often forecast. If a "good" hatch occurs, you can expect a strong year class of fish worth catching in six years when a two

Minnesota DNR conducts a walleye stripping operation every spring to raise walleyes for stocking in lakes that have poor natural reproduction.

pound plus fish would be perfect for the table. If we have an unusually cold spring, or one that is too calm or, worse yet, a bad storm that blows all the eggs or helpless fry onto dry land, the entire year class on a lake could be wiped out in a single day!

A tough life lies ahead for the walleyes that do get to this stage. Food for the fry must be available in the form of small organisms that live in abundance in nearly all lakes. As they continue to grow, their need for food changes, and if another larger food source is not found quickly, they turn to cannibalism or die. This is where perch first fit into the life of a walleye. To anglers, the perch is a pesty fish that is always willing to steal your bait: but perch are actually very important to the walleye and since the perch spawn after the walleye, the newly hatched perch fry are just the right size for the walleye fry to begin feeding on. So, in the cycle of the feeding walleye fry, nature always seems to have things planned out very well, that is until an unusual spring disrupts the plan and the perch grow too fast and are larger than the small fry can handle.

Yet, even when food is plentiful, there are predators that make survival for walleye fry a poor bet against the odds. In many cases, the odds stacked against a walleye to reproduce naturally and in sufficient numbers to sustain a good fishery often need a little help from a stocking program, or by increasing spawning habitat areas where the existing walleyes can simply help themselves in order to make better walleye fishing for everyone.

If all goes well, and the lake or river where the walleyes live has sufficient food and water to support them, the walleyes can expect a fifteen to twenty year life span.

Although walleyes have been found to survive in extreme water temperatures, the preferred temperature range for a walleye is between 55 and 69 degrees.

Walleyes come in shades of colors ranging from a dark golden color to a dull silver gray with many different shades between. Although some believe that walleyes living in shallow water tend to be lighter in color than those found in the deeper waters of the far north, we are just not sure. Many factors other than light penetration can affect their coloring, including the available food and the mineral composition of the water. A friend of mine on a recent trip to a Canadian lake caught two large walleyes from the same reef in one day. One was a dark golden color while the other was a shade of light silver.

Anglers may also find sores or warts on the sides of the walleyes, but in no way does this affect the quality of the meat. I remember once while fishing a lake near Fergus Falls, Minnesota when we had taken four beautiful walleyes while fishing for bass in the shallows. We decided to keep them for dinner that evening. When we cleaned the walleyes, we found the fillets had small worms, similar to those found in perch. It's my guess that they were feeding on the shallow water perch and since their bodies remained in the warmer waters, the walleyes got the worms from the perch. Wormy fish are often frowned upon by fishermen, but actually there is nothing wrong with the taste of the meat, and when the water temperature drops, the worms will die off. This is the reason you will often find worms in your fish fillets only during the summer months. When properly cooked the walleyes will taste just as great.

Walleye Foods

One of the most critical factors fishermen should be aware of in order to better understand where they will catch a walleye is to know what a walleye feeds on! The dominant food source in almost every lake will be different. On Mille Lacs Lake in Minnesota they feed on a minnow called a trout perch. In the Missouri River System, it's the smelt, and in the

This three pound walleye taken from the Missouri River had SEVEN smelt in his stomach when caught!

deep waters of many northern lakes, the cisco or whitefish is a prime food source.

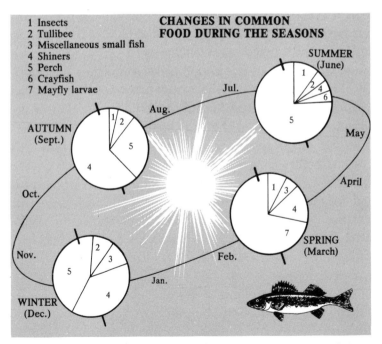

1 Insects
2 Tullibee
3 Miscellaneous small fish
4 Shiners
5 Perch
6 Crayfish
7 Mayfly larvae

CHANGES IN COMMON FOOD DURING THE SEASONS

SUMMER (June)

AUTUMN (Sept.)

May

April

SPRING (March)

WINTER (Dec.)

Jul. Aug. Oct. Nov. Jan. Feb.

The diet of a walleye changes with the season. In any one lake or river, the actual names of food may be different, but it does show how a walleye will change its feeding habits during the year.

At different times of the year walleyes change their eating habits to fit the influx of newly hatched minnows or even insects. Walleyes have been known to feed on over thirty different kinds of minnows or fish and at least as many different kinds of insects. In fact, during most of the spring and summer months it is not uncommon to find the diet of the walleye consisting almost exclusively of insects. Of

The mayfly is one of the walleye's favorite insects to eat at certain times of the year.

the insects available, the mayfly is often the most abundant.

In a later chapter, we'll explore how this predator/ prey relationship will affect your bait and lure selection. This all important relationship between predator and prey can be one of the single most important factors in finding and catching walleye. We must not forget that at times it is just about as hard to find the food source of the walleye as it is to find the walleye itself. Walleye NEVER stray far from their food. This kind of awareness is EXTREMELY important.

For the remainder of this book, I feel it's important you put aside the blinding love you may have for walleyes and realize the truth in this statement: "THE WALLEYE IS THE LAZIEST FISH THAT SWIMS." This plain and simply stated fact I'm sure will frazzle a few people, but it needs to be said.

No matter how many patches you wear on your fishing jacket or how many magazines you subscribe to, the walleye is the one who determines when "to bite or not to bite." No one can guarantee you will catch walleyes.

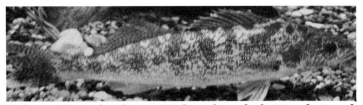

The lazy walleye often lies motionless along the bottom, but can be an effective predator when aroused to feed.

People tend to make the walleye into some super intelligent creature, but really it's almost the opposite. The walleye is a creature of his watery environment and no matter how highly we regard the walleye, nature looks at them in a different way. It's always been a lazy fish (but a classy one). When mother nature first made the walleye, she knew that everyone would soon come to love them, so she gave the walleye some very special features and habits that really make them different from all the other fish. To let the lazy walleyes feed better, she gave them the ability to see in the dark with eyes that let them feed on other fish blinded by darkness. The walleye also was given the habit of hunting for food in packs, because they can be much more successful that way.

It's amazing how things fit together like they do, all part of some master plan.

That special glowing eye of the walleye is NOT as sensitive to light as many have grown to believe. Although walleyes prefer not to experience a rapid change in light conditions, the walleye is very willing to live in shallow water as long as the food they want is present. In my travels across the country I have found that walleyes will always need three basic requirements in order to live:

1. FOOD
2. SECURITY
3. COMFORT

Of these three, FOOD is the most important factor in

Insects play a very important part in the diet of the walleye. This diagram shows how the walleye fits into a food chain as an effective predator

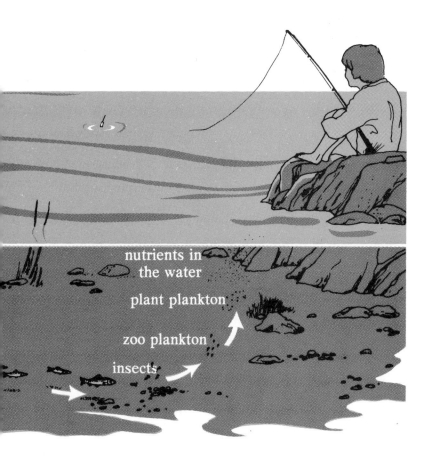

The chain of food leading to a good walleye populaton is something many anglers don't even consider. The relationship of predator to prey is often the reason for a walleye's location and feeding habits.

many lakes for locating the walleye.

In the last few years, quite a bit of noise has been made around fishing circles about finding walleyes in weeds. This discovery is in conflict with the long standing belief that walleyes love rocks, sand or gravel-bottomed areas. Walleyes in weeds are really not that strange. If we were to look at almost any of our smaller walleye lakes, it wouldn't take long to see there is very little if any textbook habitat for walleyes to live in, yet many of them do have substantial populations of walleyes. This is often the case where stocking is the only means for keeping the walleyes in the lake for anglers to catch. Walleyes really don't know where they SHOULD live, only that they require food, security and comfort. In many lakes the weeds are ideal places to live, and why not? It seems like a very logical thing for a walleye to do.

Have you ever wondered if colors really make a difference in walleye fishing? Recent studies show that the walleye CAN see colors, or at least is able to respond to color changes. The only thing we fishermen don't know is why they would prefer one color over another. To the eye of a walleye in dirty water, clear water, on bright days or at night, the most visible color is orange. Again, this does not mean walleyes will hit an orange colored bait before all others, but it has been proven to be the most visible to their eyes no matter what the conditions of the water may be.

Feeding Habits

Scuba divers often relay the same information I found from my diving experiences. The walleyes just sit on the bottom and sleep all the time. Now that you understand that the walleye is the laziest fish that swims, this fact shouldn't come as any big surprise.

Walleye are predator fish, but for years people

thought they were finicky eaters who nibble on baits and always play hard to get, so to catch a walleye you really have to be careful about watching for strikes. My logic for walleyes is really simple, because when you come right down to it, a walleye wouldn't survive long if it went around nibbling the tails off the minnows it wanted to eat. Walleye are gulpers, NOT nibblers! I know this statement may confuse many anglers who have fallen victim to a half-eaten nightcrawler or minnow and are convinced that each missed fish was a fifteen pound walleye. Life for the walleye fisherman would be a lot better if they followed the advice given to me by a veteran river fisherman. "If that walleye was big enough to keep, he would have easily grabbed your bait right down to his gut!"

If you went around thinking every fish you missed was a keeper, you would soon be frustrated into thinking that you are jinxed. The thing to realize is that smaller, more aggressive fish often peck at a bait that is nearly impossible for them to swallow, but they often have high hopes of swallowing it anyway. Of course, you will run into the rare exception to the rule when big walleyes are very, very lazy. Anglers should be aware that the size of your bait is VERY critical in your trying to get the attention of the kind of walleye you want to keep. This is when some of the little tricks I will be talking about later in the book can really pay off with some big stringers.

Walleye Movements

Walleye movements are often the grounds for debate among anglers, but the importance of how walleyes get from one area to another is really not as great as many would like to think. It's much more important to know what to do to get the walleyes to hit when you find them. In many shallow water lakes where the depth very

22

seldom exceeds thirty feet, you will often find walleyes making horizontal movements to and from feeding areas. In deep lakes, walleyes tend to move more up and down in order to reach their feeding areas. These lakes often have lots of water fifty feet or more in depth. River walleyes move horizontally as well, but with a special regard to current and water levels. These migrations from holding to feeding areas often occur when weather and light conditions are ideal. If we were to look at all the variables that control when and why walleyes feed, this book would need to be different for every lake and river system.

There has been a big push lately about charts that can predict when the fishing will be the best. This has got to be one of the most consistently asked questions when I'm giving seminars, and I always give the same answer. It goes like this: "I love to fish, and if I plan on going fishing, I'm going fishing. No fancy chart or moon phase is going to decide for me when I can and cannot catch fish. About the time you start believing in them, you get into a huge stringer of fish during the worst

This Wisconsin limit of walleye was taken in conditions far from "ideal." No one really knows what fish will do all the time.

possible times. Local weather conditions are much more important than some chart for predicting when the fish will be feeding. Besides, I'd rather be fishing than cutting the grass at home anytime!"

Using the general differences between deep lakes, shallow lakes and then rivers, I wish to give you a sample of how walleyes will behave differently so you, the fisherman, may want to adjust your fishing times or location to increase your success ratio. There are countless combinations that could be plugged into the chart, but for our purpose, the use of the most commonly found conditions will give you a better idea of how to select a lake that could be in a productive mood.

Of the conditions listed on the chart on pages twenty-four and twenty-five, the cold front is the worst enemy of the walleye fisherman. Walleyes are the most susceptible of all gamefish to the effects of a cold front.

Local weather conditions can greatly affect the feeding patterns of walleye.

To recognize a cold front condition, remember:
1. Cold fronts often follow a major storm.
2. Cold fronts create a rapid temperature drop.
3. Cold fronts are followed by a blue bird day and often a breeze.

What turns the fish so consistently off their feeding

The Effects of Weather

Description:	SUNNY DAYS	CLOUDY DAYS
DEEP LAKES Clear, 90 feet deep plus. Very large walleyes, but not many. Sand and rock bottom. Steep drops into deep water.	Walleyes tend to move deeper, feeding at dawn and dusk but mostly during the night.	Increases the chances of finding walleyes in a more aggressive mood all day due to the decrease in light penetration.
SHALLOW LAKES Dirty, 30 ft. max. Fair size walleyes but the quantity is above average. Muck and sand bottom with very gradual drops.	Although the water is still bright because of the sun, walleyes will be more willing to feed later into the day.	Walleyes will stay shallow for longer periods and are often catchable.
RIVERS Stained, 10 ft. average depth. Small to fair size walleyes, and not very abundant. Mostly sand and muck bottom.	Walleyes move tighter to bottom or tight to obstructions in order to be more comfortable. Will feed at any time.	Walleyes will to roam areas away from cover which will make them easier to get a lure to.

Conditions on Walleyes

RAIN AND WIND	NIGHT TIME	COLD FRONTS
If you're a daytime angler these times can often give you the best action of all. Walleyes can be found very shallow at this time.	The best time to find feeding walleyes on a lake like this. Many believe that this is the only time when walleyes can be consistently caught in shallow water.	This type of lake is the most affected by fronts and fishing could be shut down almost completely!
If not too extreme in either case, walleyes will be very aggressive all day because rain and wave action reduce light penetration even more.	Your best times will be the two hours before and after twilight. Walleyes will move to the shallows and feed very heavily.	This type of lake can offer the only action you will find when a front moves in. But fishing is still very difficult.
Increased water levels could get the walleyes to feed if not too drastic a storm. Can also be an excellent place to fish if other lakes are too windy.	Night fishing for walleyes is rare, simply because walleyes can be so consistently caught during the daylight hours. The twilight hours are your best bet.	River fish are the least affected of all waters by fronts, but this still means you will need to work for your fish.

habits is something we really know nothing about. Sure, there are theories about how insects or barometric pressure might affect the walleyes, but nobody knows for sure yet. A guideline I use for working with cold fronts is that the clearer the water you are fishing, the longer it could take to recover. Three days is the normal time needed, but it could take up to five days if the lake is unusually clear and deep. Many people believe that the walleyes go deep when a cold front moves through. This statement is somewhat true, but more than anything, you must realize that the walleyes become dormant. They could sink into a thick weedbed or lie motionless in 10, 20 or 50 feet of water. The old expression of having "lock jaw" is a great term to describe a walleye during this cold front condition.

One midwestern walleye tournament held a few years back was right after the worst cold front you could ever imagine. After two hard days of fishing, the two hundred anglers came back to the docks without a single walleye! Not even the professionals can find the answers to catching fish during a cold front.

EFFECTS OF WAVE ACTION

This obvious but commonly overlooked act of nature is one very good way of attracting concentrations of minnows to one small area. The reduction of light created by the waves will often give the walleye the extra edge it likes when feeding. Ideally, you will want to always try wind-blown shorelines. This wave action increases walleye's feeding activity if the wind blows from the same direction for 48 hours or more. It often takes this long for a definite feeding pattern to be established. If a sudden storm blows in, the effect of wave action may not be noticeable. This is especially true if the wind starts blowing from a completely

Wave action can easily bring the super big walleyes into the shallows during the day.

different direction.

I can remember a "do or die" situation for catching a big walleye when I was hired to produce one seven pound walleye for a television commercial. I was given only one day to catch it, which makes for a real challenge. The day dawned with a howling wind of 30 mph from the north. My plan was to catch that walleye from a popular walleye hotspot called Mille Lacs Lake, about 100 miles north of my Minneapolis home, and ship it back to town alive the following morning. Mille Lacs is one of the biggest wind traps in Minnesota, and no walleye is worth risking my life to catch. I put my hopes on the wind letting up in the evening. By seven the wind was down to 15 mph, so it was off to the nearest windswept rock point I could find. Not more than a quarter mile from the boat ramp a beautiful eight pound walleye hit a Rapala on my tenth cast right on top of the shallow reef in only two feet of water! I was relieved, to say the least, but if I hadn't played the wind properly it could have taken many days to find that soon-to-be-famous walleye.

Wave action, even under the most severe weather conditions, can be a big help in getting the walleyes moving again. This is especially true when a cold front really shuts fishing down. Anglers often curse the wind, as I often do myself because it can really make fishing very difficult. With a safe boat and a little common sense, walleye fishing on a windy day can be a rewarding experience.

SUSPENDED WALLEYES VS. BOTTOM WALLEYES

One of the newest trends, or maybe I should say fads, in walleye fishing stems from the finding that walleyes float or suspend in open water and often great distances above the bottom. In my travels to Lake Erie I found that here the walleyes do spend a great portion of their time suspended ten feet or more above the bottom. Why? For years people thought that walleyes preferred the bottom in rock, gravel, or sandy areas. Just when it seems that we were getting the hang of finding the walleyes, you, the fisherman, get thrown a curve and you begin to think you have been fishing in the wrong places. Well folks, don't despair, walleyes DO like to live on the bottom and in only a few lakes will this not be the case. These suspended walleyes are mostly found in large shallow bodies of water like Erie or Mille Lacs. In these lakes walleyes suspend for the obvious reasons of getting the food, comfort and security that all fish would like to have. There is no mystery to why they suspend, only the problem of trying to figure out how to catch them. I definitely have a few tricks for you to try later in the book for catching these suspended fish.

For now, let me say I don't want everyone to think all walleyes suspend. They most definitely DO NOT and if you are looking to start catching more walleyes this season, you had better start believing it, too. The best and most consistent place to find old marble eyes is right near the bottom. Walleyes by nature relate to the bottom of the lake when they rest and feed. It's nice to make a revolutionary breakthrough for catching suspended walleyes, but if it works only once or twice in a lifetime, I'm really not doing too much to help increase your success overall, because you'll be wasting lots of money and effort until you stumble on the occasion where you just might take a few fish on that new razzle-dazzle technique. The basic rule for walleyes still holds true today; for consistent catches it's best to ALWAYS stay near the bottom.

This beautiful ten pound walleye was taken by simply dragging the bait along the bottom. For consistent success it's often a good rule to stay within two feet of the bottom at all times.

Lakes and Rivers Walleye Love

With extensive stocking and the introduction of walleyes into many new parts of the country, the walleye boom is growing fast. In the last twenty years the additional habitat created by man-made reservoirs has produced some of the finest walleye fishing in the world! The best example of this is the great walleye fishing found in the Missouri River System.

Having sampled walleye fishing all over the country, I am not only impressed with the quantity of the fish taken from the Missouri River System, but also the size.

An angler fishing Lake Erie puts on ice another fine eating size walleye.

In Lake Erie, another fantastic walleye area, a five pound fish is considered an excellent fish with limits of two to three pound walleyes very common. In the Missouri River on Lake Sakakawea, however, you can expect a five pounder to be AVERAGE during most of the fishing season. How long this kind of fishing will continue is still unknown. Even fisheries people can't give a definite answer because there is no other fishery quite like it anywhere else. In a later chapter I have included a special section for anglers who may plan on traveling to these areas.

Lakes and rivers are like people—each has its own special features which make it unique. To put lakes and rivers into a lot of special categories would just confuse most anglers. It is therefore impossible and unneccesary to make specific statements about "ALL" kinds of similar water. The best we can do is to start with a general guideline to help put things in better perspective.

FACT: Lakes and rivers DO grow old.

This statement is not revolutionary, but the understanding of how lakes grow older can put them into or out of the potential of being a prime walleye producing body of water. Most lakes and rivers fit into one of three major age groups.

YOUNG WATER Water here is clear and often drinkable. These waters often have rocky bottoms, are very deep and are typical of a Canadian wilderness lake. Walleyes here are often few in numbers, but these waters can produce very large fish if the angling pressure has not been too severe. When fishermen or commercial netting has harvested the larger fish, these lakes will have an abundant supply of one and two pound fish that never seem to grow. Fish movements are often up and down steep drop-offs to deeper water which are commonly found in this type of lake. These lakes are often irregular in shape with many islands and are the most directly affected by cold fronts.

The best way of defining a young river is simply to call it a babbling brook. A small shallow stream has little or no potential for holding walleyes except in areas where it may flow into a lake.

MIDDLE-AGED WATER Waters that fall into this category have mostly sand or gravel bottoms. They

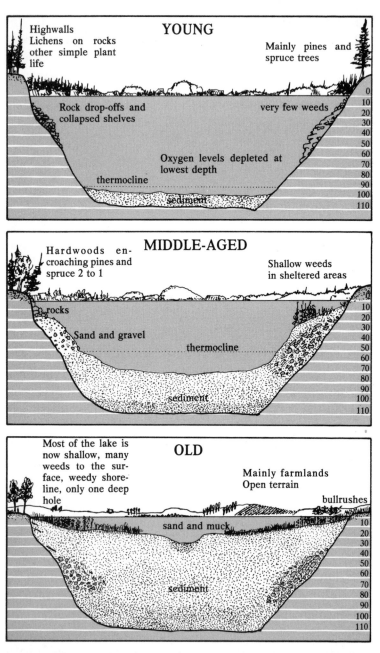

YOUNG

Highwalls Lichens on rocks other simple plant life

Mainly pines and spruce trees

Rock drop-offs and collapsed shelves

very few weeds

Oxygen levels depleted at lowest depth

thermocline

sediment

0
10
20
30
40
50
60
70
80
90
100
110

MIDDLE-AGED

Hardwoods encroaching pines and spruce 2 to 1

Shallow weeds in sheltered areas

rocks

Sand and gravel

thermocline

sediment

0
10
20
30
40
50
60
70
80
90
100
110

OLD

Most of the lake is now shallow, many weeds to the surface, weedy shoreline, only one deep hole

Mainly farmlands Open terrain

bullrushes

sand and muck

sediment

10
20
30
40
50
60
70
80
90
100
110

LIFE CYCLE OF A LAKE

have an area of deep water, but the average depth is usually under 30 feet with a maximum depth of under 100 feet. Visibility is often two to five feet and these types of waters can often produce both quality and quantity walleye fishing. They are considered to be ideal waters for a natural supply of walleye to exist.

A "stream" with mostly sand and gravel bottoms would best describe the middle-aged river. Natural reproduction is often good and fishing pressure is often light, so these waters should have a plentiful supply of walleyes.

OLD WATER These are often small lakes that have mud or silt covering most of the bottom. Visibility is often limited to only inches. Walleyes would not naturally be here, but stocking programs often make walleye fishing possible. Quantity fishing is very seldom found, but the fish are often large because of the warmer, fertile water which permits them to grow quickly. These lakes are least affected by cold fronts. Such lakes unfortunately are often victims of oxygen depletion during severe winters—a condition that can literally kill ALL the fish.

The mighty Mississippi River is a perfect example of an old river. Often slow and dirty, these river systems have mostly sand and muck bottoms. Although such rivers do have occasional rocky areas to hold walleye, they are rare. In many older rivers man has built additional rocky areas called wingdams to increase current flow and improve navigational routes. The walleyes found here often grow quite large, but are not plentiful. Certain stretches of river that contain natural reproduction areas may produce better than other areas lacking the vital needs of the walleye.

Although further classification of lake and river types may better serve the fisheries biologists, these are the three major categories of water important for you to

34

recognize. The progression from young to old takes thousands of years, and only recently has the introduction of man-made fertilizers and other forms of pollution increased the speed of this aging process. With proper environmental management, many lakes and rivers can bounce back from this accelerated aging; some, however, cannot. Increased pollution in our lakes and rivers benefits no one but the carp.

For years people have sought a secret to better fishing success. Well folks, I'm about to shed some new light on a fact I know will mean more and even bigger walleyes than you have ever caught before. For years this has been the secret "advantage" for the pro's. Are you longing to hoist a limit of lunker walleyes?

ZENANKO'S RULE FOR MORE WALLEYES: To catch more walleyes, fish a lake known for having lots of walleyes in it!

Stop and think for a minute about the truth in

To catch walleyes like this, you shouldn't waste your time on lakes known better for bass or northern pike. Selecting the right lake can make all the difference.

this statement. Anglers spend thousands of hours fishing for walleyes on lakes that have so few of them in the first place. It's like looking for a needle in a haystack!! SURE, you can catch them and SURE, there are some real lunkers out there, but let's tell it like it is folks. Do you want to FISH for walleyes or CATCH walleyes? By fishing lakes and rivers that have a high concentration of walleyes, the tips and techniques you'll be reading about in the rest of this book will do you some good. If you continue to fish lakes that are rumored to have walleyes in them, don't expect this book to be much help.

Remember our three major water types? Try to avoid fishing old waters, fish the middle-aged waters for the numbers and the young waters for the lunkers. With this in mind, when fishing these waters, everyone would like to consistently catch nice walleyes with an occasional trophy thrown in, so read on. . .

WALLEYE LOCATIONS IN LAKES

A very important factor in finding walleyes stems from the predator/prey relationships we have already talked briefly about. Now I'd like to stress the importance of how finding the food source can be the key to finding walleye.

It is important to realize that the feeding habits of walleyes WILL change during the basic seasons of spring, summer, fall and winter. Let's follow a group of walleyes on a typical middle-aged lake through the course of a year.

SPRING This is spawning time and the one time in which the basic principles of walleye fishing can go right out the window. The spawning instincts will draw the fish shallow and although we would all like to catch a trophy walleye early in the season, the bigger females are loners as each fish waits in deeper water while her eggs ripen. Anglers often do well around the mouths of rivers, but much of the early season walleyes can also be found along long shallow points or shorelines in two to ten feet of water. The important factor here is to search for gravel or small rocks about the size of softballs or less. Walleyes can often be found in such areas in great numbers, although the majority of them will be the small one to three pound males.

Fishing at night may increase your chances of

These Red Wing area walleyes were caught in open water in early March. The weather may be cold and miserable, but your fishing success can be rewarding.

catching a big female when she first enters the shallow spawning areas. Big females very seldom feed when they are actually spawning and your time might be better spent fishing for the less impressive but more aggressive males. Some states have waters which are open year-around for all species. One such area is the Mississippi River along the Minnesota/Wisconsin border near the town of Red Wing, Minnesota. For the last several years there has been a big controversy about having the season open all year in this area. To try to find out the effects of having no seasonal restrictions on fishing, the Minnesota and Wisconsin DNR (Department of Natural Resources) worked on a project for five years to find out if the walleye fishing was being hurt. The end result of the study showed that the walleyes here have not been affected by the pressures of year-round angling. This is not to say that we should eliminate seasons for game fish, but in this one case the angling pressure has not hurt this walleye fishery.

I do however, sincerely believe that fishing on many lakes can be very badly damaged if the spawning fish are not left alone. Ideally the best time to find concentrations of big female walleyes is just before they spawn. Many anglers frown on angling at this time because the egg laying potential of those females could play a big part in the future of walleye populations in a lake.

One such occasion was when the new Minnesota state record walleye was taken from the Seagull River a few years back. That year we had a very late thaw in Minnesota, and normally the DNR would have closed this area to protect the females during spawning. Opening weekend came just as the females moved out of Lake Saganaga and into the Seagull River. Literally hundreds of ten pound plus walleyes were caught or

Catching these big pre-spawn females when they are grouped together in early spring may have an effect on the walleye population in that lake in years to come.

snagged during the first two nights of the season. Some say that up to 80 percent of the spawners were taken during those first two days! If true, future fishing success will be drastically reduced in three to six years.

When spawning has been completed, fishermen often find that fishing is far below what they had expected. This is due to a combination of factors you may have no control over. Being a successful spring season walleye angler often means you must spend a great portion of your time fishing at night! One of the most important factors in this night time walleye activity is simply the force of habit! You already learned in the first chapter that a walleye can migrate 200 miles to reach a spawning area, but did you know that the majority of this movement takes place at night? That's right! For the last month or more, the walleyes have been moving, feeding and spawning at night. Their habits of night time activity will still dominate their lives for up to a month after spawning.

Right after spawning has been completed, many anglers will find the big fish simply disappear. Female walleyes have really gone through a lot in the last few weeks and need some time to simply let their bodies recuperate. This is something we fishermen have little control over and until the water begins to warm and the females decide it's time to start feeding again, the smaller male walleyes will make up 95% of the catch.

A typical stringer of opening day walleye. In this catch, all the walleyes were males from 1½ to 3 pounds.

As the waters begin to warm, the feeding needs of the walleye will increase so that they will also be needing to feed during the day. This time of year is often considered the best fishing of the year.

SUMMERTIME WALLEYE LOCATION

As the bigger walleye start feeding more and more during the day, packs or schools of walleye begin to take shape. Fish of the same age class tend to school together, so it is very common to fish one spot and catch fish that all seem to be running the same size. A school of walleyes could consist of 10, 20 or 200 fish depending on the age of the fish and the lake you are fishing.

I wish there were some universal habits that all walleyes exhibit during the summer months, but depending on where you live, their habits differ. This is where the predator/prey relationship can send walleyes on one lake into fifty feet of water looking for smelt or ciscos, while on the other side of the road the walleyes are feeding on emerging insects just below the surface. How on earth am I going to list every possibility for you to try, knowing full well that things could change in a day, hour, or in even minutes? Walleyes are predator fish, and their taste buds and habits will change without letting you know about it. The best I can do is recommend places walleyes are most often found and caught.

Summer walleyes often relate to two commonly found sites—POINTS and ISLANDS. An obvious shoreline point should never be overlooked when fishing a new lake. Wave action in combination with the change of the shoreline's shape often tends to hold walleyes nearby and will offer a quick and easy place to

Isolated islands of any size can be a great place to start looking for walleye.

begin fishing. In my younger days, if I really wanted to catch walleyes, the big trick was to simply find a drop-off any old place and fish. This was an area where the bottom of the lake drops off to deeper water. In many of our lakes the drop-off will serve as a highway for walleyes to move along. In this vein of thought, points act as an intersection where they can move upwards into the shallows when the conditions are right. The depth at which these fish move from one place to another will vary every day.

On a clear, calm day they SHOULD be deeper along the break to deeper water. On a cloudy or windy day they SHOULD be shallower because of the reduced sunlight penetration. Thus, the less light you have, the shallower you should fish and conversely, the more light you have, the deeper you should fish.

Isolated islands are one of my favorite places to find walleyes on new lakes. One of the reasons for this is that an isolated island is what I like to consider, a miniature lake all in itself. Fishing a large Canadian lake like Lake Of The Woods along the Minnesota/Canadian border can be an awesome task. The lake is mile after mile of islands and reefs. The big secret to fishing these big lakes is to select only a few islands and zero in on the walleyes that live around them. Within a very short time you can learn the bottom contours of the lake around those islands and find fish. Ideally, I would like to select islands with long tapering points on them or ones that are near areas of water 20 feet deep or less. Islands with steep breaks all around them simply do not have enough fishable water to make it worth your effort.

Fishing just any old spot along a shoreline is at best a gamble and it would be sheer luck if you stumble into a school of fish. Anglers are always best advised to start fishing points and islands when they begin fishing a new body of water.

Walleyes in the weeds? The reasons why walleyes in some lakes live in the weeds stem from the basic requirements all fish have for food, security and comfort. As a walleye adjusts to the environment, anglers should adjust as well if they hope to have any success at all. This seems like just as good a time as any to let you know yet another secret to catching more walleyes consistently. "YOU must go to the walleye and not wait for the walleye to come to you!"

At no time is this statement more true than with weed walleyes. Many lakes located near metropolitan areas are often heavily stocked with walleyes. The lake itself is often not capable of supporting a population of walleye without extensive stocking. The end result is a lake without typical walleye structure like rock bars or even hard bottoms. These lakes are often very "stained" by heavy amounts of algae. The walleyes still need food, security and comfort and the weeds are the logical place for them to live. I can remember one bass tournament I was fishing in southern Minnesota. The lake was just one step away from being a swamp. The water was so dirty you could only see into it a few inches at best. On this day the walleyes were actively feeding in the lily pads in only two feet of water! That day we took more walleye than bass unfortunately, but we did catch walleyes up to eight pounds!

This beautiful eight pound walleye was taken on a Buzz Bullet spinnerbait by Denny Martin while fishing bass in lily pads!

FALL WALLEYES The fall fishing season usually begins as the first heavy frost hits the leaves. This transition from summer feeding patterns to fall habits is one of the hardest times for the walleye and the walleye fisherman as well. The big trick to consistent walleye catches is just plain good timing. Lakes will continue to cool in the fall until the surface temperature is the same as the temperature at the bottom of the lake. At this time the lake turns over and often stirs up the water for a week or longer. "Turnover" is a very important change a lake must go through every season to mix-up water temperatures and oxygen levels. There is a turnover every spring too, but during the spring

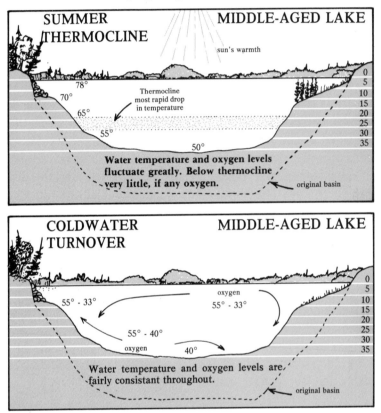

SUMMER THERMOCLINE   **MIDDLE-AGED LAKE**

sun's warmth

78°
70°
65°
55°

Thermocline most rapid drop in temperature

50°

Water temperature and oxygen levels fluctuate greatly. Below thermocline very little, if any oxygen.

original basin

0
5
10
15
20
25
30
35

COLDWATER TURNOVER   **MIDDLE-AGED LAKE**

55° - 33°
oxygen
55° - 33°

55° - 40°

oxygen
40°

Water temperature and oxygen levels are fairly consistant throughout.

original basin

0
5
10
15
20
25
30
35

turnover, spawning activity is a bigger thing. Fishing a lake while it's turning over is tough, because the world of the walleye is all mixed up and they are now free to roam to any depth they wish on a lake. You will need to either fish a larger lake or a deeper one that may take longer to cool off, or simply wait until the lake has settled before you can expect to find the walleyes. With good timing you can fish a small lake early in the fall until you notice the turnover starting, then switch to a larger lake which will often not start to turn over for a week or more. This is a great technique to continue catching fish into the fall months.

Fall is considered the best time of year to catch a hawg walleye. One of the main reasons for this is that the female fish have been feeding heavily and are heavily laden with eggs for next spring. Over the winter months the colder water temperatures will limit the amount of egg growth.

As the weed beds begin to die off, most of the baitfish in a lake shift to sandy or rocky areas to feed. When the food shifts to a new location, so does the walleye. A consistent trick for finding fall walleyes is to seek out the steepest drop-offs on the lake near shore. This is often a popular haunt for walleyes because it offers the quickest possible route to reach their feeding areas

Time and time again the preference walleyes have for feeding during the low light times of dawn and dusk is very noticeable. When walleyes feed, you can be finding them in three to ten feet of water. The problem is that during the day they could be resting in thirty to fifty feet of water! Anglers not aware of these rapid depth changes often experience extremely good fishing or extremely poor fishing success.

Steep drop-offs near shore can produce a quick stringer of BIG walleyes in the fall.

One nice thing about fall fishing is that once you know an area where the walleye are feeding, you have often found a consistent place to find walleyes until the ice has formed over the lake.

WINTER WALLEYE Since the walleye's metabolism is controlled by water temperature, the best angling will occur in the first month after the ice has

These mid-winter river fishermen slide their boat across the ice to reach open water. . . .

But as you can see, all of their extra effort DID pay off big!

formed over the lake. As water temperatures continue to drop during the sub-zero temperatures of late January and February, so does walleye activity. Snow cover can be a big asset to a successful ice fishing season. Under a blanket of snow that keeps the sunlight from penetrating the ice, the walleyes can roam in very shallow water during the day.

The locations for feeding walleye often do not vary much from areas where you will find them in late fall. The big difference is that the walleyes will often prefer to stay much deeper. What seems to be happening here is that the perch move from the shallows and look for hard bottomed areas of sand in about thirty feet of water. Since the perch is often the favorite food for the walleye in many lakes, their shift to holding all day in deep water is now no big mystery. A walleye living in cold water does not need to feed as often or for long periods as they would in the heat of the summer, but the predator/prey relationship is still a big factor in their lives.

Selecting a Rod and Reel for Walleye

The selection of a properly balanced rod and reel combination is far more important to the walleye fisherman than most realize, and you won't need to mortgage the house to buy one. Having been in the fishing tackle retail business for five years, I have seen some strange outfits people have been buying to use for walleye and it upset me to think that they would be actually trying to catch a fish with a mis-matched outfit. As a salesman, it was always my goal to put anglers into a balanced outfit which they could afford. Many many manufactors for example, offer a series of fiberglass rods that are designed very well for walleye fishing and sell for about $15. Several reel companies make some very reliable spinning reels that sell for under $25. A walleye fisherman would be able to enjoy the sport much better with this balanced $40 outfit than if he invested $150 in a mis-matched one.

The walleye outfits I sold had three different price ranges, depending upon how many frills you wanted. In the ranges of $50, $100 and $150, each had some very good selling points. One outfit may have more durable line guides, another a high quality cork handle and still another might be a two piece rod with a handsome case for storage.

Walleye fishermen today really have been brain-washed by some rod manufacturers into believing that their ability to feel vibrations in a rod is essential to better fishing. Baloney! It really burns me up to think people actually believe a rod that transmits vibrations down its shaft is a better walleye rod. Many rod companies get into big debates on which rod material or design is best. This can really cause some confusion for consumers because they really don't know who to believe. Fiberglass used in fishing rods is considered a cheap rod material. Graphite is a fairly new material for fishing rods and is lighter and much stronger than fiberglass. It is the most popular selling rod material on the market today. Boron is the newest and most expensive material to be used for rods in recent years. It is said to be lighter and stronger than graphite and is the choice of the "experts." HA!!! For as long as I can remember, fishermen have always been into fads and gimmicks looking for the extra edge in catching more walleyes. To really put this little game manufacturers play with fishermen into better perspective, we have to just stop and think about how many more fish you will catch with a $200 rod than with one costing only $20.

It's time someone speaks out and tells it like it is, because too many people are throwing money away on expensive rods. During the past ten years I have had a chance to use nearly every kind of rod on the market. Each claims to be the most sensitive, lightest, strongest or best designed. Anglers must realize that cost does not reflect the way it will perform on the water. To me, this performance factor is very important. When it comes right down to it, feeling the vibrations in a rod is a bunch of hogwash! Rods need to be sensitive, yes, but not in the way rod makers advertise them. An ad would often read something like this. "Vibrations travel through our graphite rod 173.4 times faster than through a comparable fiberglass model." Salesmen often ask folks to hold the handle of the rod while they rub the tip against the wall to see if you can feel the vibrations. I shudder everytime I see this done, because vibrations are not what the fisherman will be feeling when a strike occurs. The single most important factor in a good walleye rod is WEIGHT! This is where the newer rod materials like graphite and boron really excel. The best kept secret in putting together a good walleye rod is the weight of the rod itself. That is why a cheap $15 rod with thin tubular walls can work very well in some actions for walleye fishing. The big problem here is that many of these cheap rods are really not designed to last. They may also lack many of the nice features that come standard on more expensive rods.

Graphite is where the rod industry is putting a real push to get you to buy. This space-age material was the talk of the town when it first hit the market. The rods were extremely expensive and earned a reputation for breaking easily. Today this material is almost as cheap as fiberglass, and newer methods of production have made it one of the toughest rod materials ever to be developed. The lighter weight of a graphite rod is a real advantage over a fiberglass rod. The Fenwick Company makes the Eagle series of graphite rods that sell for a price well below many other graphites, but lack only the cosmetic differences of the $100 models, and are still covered with a lifetime guarantee.

Boron is the newest rod material to hit the market in recent years. It is a material stronger yet lighter in

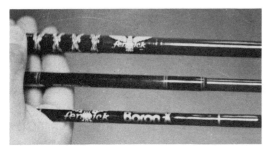

Here are three identical rod designs in three different materials: fiberglass on top, graphite and then boron. Note the obvious differences in the diameters of the rod shafts. You can visually see the difference from fiberglass to graphite, but the graphite to boron is not that significant.

weight than graphite. This super material is not
without its problems, though. Many rod companies try
to make boron rods by cutting corners and blending it
with graphite and still calling it a boron rod to help sell
it. Granted, some graphite needs to be in each of these
boron rods to help the material remain bonded
together, but when it comes right down to it, you will
only notice a slight difference between a quality
graphite rod and a boron one. In many cases, the extra
price you pay will not be worth it, unless you like to
impress your friends.

All right, WEIGHT not VIBRATIONS is the key
factor when looking for a new walleye rod. The tip of
the rod you select must be flexible as well. One good
way to check this is NOT to shake the rod in the tackle
shop trying the feel the action, but to ask the salesman
to put a line on the rod so you can see how it flexes. I
have found that most good walleye rods have nearly all
of the action or flex in the top 1/3 of the rod. Your rod
tip needs to VISUALLY tell you what is going on.

Your monofilament fishing line acts like a long
rubber band that stretches whenever any weight is put
on it. Then you have water resistance which creates
slack in your line. The vibrations of a strike may be
great, but are quickly dulled to a sensation of increased
weight. This is something that must be seen visually in
many cases. A big advantage with a lightweight
graphite rod really comes into play now because you
may notice a slight increase in weight that even your
rod tip may have a hard time showing. Many times a
strike will feel as though you have hooked a weed.
Being able to sense this increase in weight does take
practice. That is why I suggest you watch your rod tip
at all times for a strike. I've seen charter boat captains
on some lakes ask their clients to simply lean their rods
against the side of the boat and wait until the deck hand

tells you to set the hook. With just a glance it's possible to watch a dozen rods at a time for strikes! Having that rod tip flexible is vital to your ability to detect a strike. Advertising, however, is a powerful force that many people believe as the gospel truth. Take for example, the rods that are claimed to be 100% graphite. To be 100% graphite, the thickness of the rod blank itself has to be almost the same from butt to tip. This will make for a rod that is extremely tip heavy. I often refer to rods like this as being "war clubs." A rod that flexes only in the bottom 2/3 of the blank leaves the rod tip stiff and heavy. Oh, sure, the material might be scientifically more sensitive to vibrations, but it lacks the action best suited for walleye fishing. Of course, if the angler never has had a chance to see what a good walleye rod feels like, they may never miss the advantages. In this case, it will just take a little longer to develop a good sense of feel and control of the line.

Note the flex of this spinning rod. The action is found in the top one-third of the rod.

These guidelines for selecting a walleye rod are surprisingly universal for nearly any length rod you may select. There are enough manufacturers of rods these days to really give you a good variety to choose from.

LONG RODS VS. SHORT RODS

There is a time and a place for every rod on the market today. You, the angler, must personally decide on the way in which you plan to do most of your walleye fishing, because rod length can make a difference in your ability to fish certain areas.

For short range fishing, 35 feet or closer to the boat, I

prefer to use a 5¼ to 5½ foot rod. Shorter rods used here give you much better line control and casting accuracy. The farther you plan on fishing from the boat or shore the longer the rod you should be using. The biggest advantage with longer rods is a stronger hookset at longer distances. Simply put, you can take up more slack line with a single pull of a long rod, which makes for fewer missed fish. A long rod is considered to be 6½ to 7 feet.

Specialty rods make up another rod type to choose from. They could be very strong rods for trolling artifical lures as are often used on the Missouri River System. These rods are likely to be baitcasting or heavy spinning rods that can handle twenty pound test line. With this kind of fishing, weight is not at all critical because artificial lures are often used.

When purchasing a new rod you must also decide if you want a one or two piece model. The advantage with a one piece rod is in having better flexing action with less weight and more strength. Two or more pieces in the design of a rod increases the number of "dead spots" in the flex of the rod which may result in untimely breakage. Of course if you are in need of a rod that can fit into the trunk of your car, the choice has already been made. In this case, avoid rods with metal ferrules which drastically decrease the rod's action. Two piece rods are also more expensive to manufacture, and thus are priced significantly higher than a one piece rod of comparable length.

Rod guides are another important consideration for selecting a quality rod. This may seem a bit trivial at first, but any good rod maker will tell you that the guides you select for a rod can make or break its action. The aluminum-oxide guides that are very popular today for reducing line wear can add unnecessary weight and stiffness to the shaft of a rod. A big breakthrough in guides was recently made with the introduction of the single foot guides. Older style guides still work on the stiff rod actions, but if you want

a rod with lots of flex the two footed guides would actually restrict the flex of the rod. The tying of a two footed guide onto a rod blank would create a series of miniature dead spots. A single foot guide flexes nicely with the rod blank and can permit you to lessen the total weight of the finished rod. Every season newer space-aged materials have made rod

The very durable single foot guides offer rods a much more natural flex.

guides lighter and even stronger, but for now at least, the cost of these newer guides will prohibit them from being put on all but the most expensive rods.

REELS

Spinning tackle is without a doubt the best choice for walleye fishing nine out of ten times. Many anglers who have never used spinning tackle or have had a bad experience with spinning tackle will fail to see the reasons why it can be a big advantage in your fishing. Let's take a look at the reasons why spinning tackle is so popular:

1. DOMINANT HAND Most anglers have much better feel and more strength in their right hand (if they are right handed). Better coordination in their dominant hand will provide better control of their casts and lure action.

2. LIGHT LINES No other reel type is capable of holding and casting light lines. Ideal for live bait fishermen because they will get greater distances without losing their baits as easily.

3. LIGHT LURES Open face spinning reels truly excel when you find a need to cast a light lure a long distance. This was a luxury that anglers have long wanted out of a fishing reel, but never could get.

Spinning reels are your best all-around choice for walleye fishing.

Spinning reels come in many different price ranges and often the price you pay reflects the features you will get. A 20 to 30 dollar reel can do the job very nicely. If you are in doubt as to which reel to select, follow these guidelines:

1. SMOOTHNESS A simple check of turning the reel handle should signal any unnecessary vibration, grinding or wobbling of the reel's action. This could easily distract you from detecting a strike when it occurs.

2. WEIGHT Again weight is important. If it is a toss-up on which reel to take, select the one which weighs the least. After holding the reel that has only a few extra ounces for twelve hours or so, you will soon wish you had selected the lighter

weight model.
3. SERVICE Are parts and service close by so you can get it fixed WHEN it breaks down? ALL reels have parts that will eventually wear out, but if you buy a model that hasn't been made in five years and try to find parts, it may be best to just buy a whole new reel!

BALANCING YOUR OUTFIT

Selecting a rod and reel combination by random and calling it a balanced outfit is a common error made by novice anglers. Balancing an outfit that is right for you takes planning. First, you must decide what kind of walleye fishing you plan on doing. Let's say you do most of your fishing with ¼ ounce jigs and you prefer short rods. Look on the rod rack of your local tackle shop and set aside all the spinning rods 5½ feet and under. By looking at the shaft of the rod just above the handle, you will find the manufacturer's rod specifications which tell you what lure weights this rod will best handle. Once you've narrowed the field of rods off the rack to this point you often only have a few to select from. Now your own personal preferences can come into play to help make a final decision. Things like cost, rod material, type of guides, warranty or even the color of the rod itself may influence your final decision.

In the reel category, you must look to see what weight lines this new rod can handle. With any reel, there is a line size best suited to give maximum performance. This information is often found right on the box or on the spool of the reel itself. For example, the best rod and reel combination would have the following specifications:

ROD: Length 5¼ ft. Lures ⅛ to ½ oz.
Recommended line size 4 to 10 lbs.

REEL: Recommended line sizes 4 to 6 lb. test.
LINE: Load reel with 6 lbs. test line.
The total amount of money you plan on spending is
entirely up to you, because there is a wide variety of
price ranges available for the fisherman of today. I
would like to again remind anglers that the extra price
you may pay for a fancy rod and reel outfit will not
catch the fish for you. YOU will still have to do that.

MONOFILAMENT LINE

In the post war years manufacturers started looking
for peace-time applications for an important war-time
creation. Today, nylon is a household word and is the
major ingredient in monofilament fishing lines.
Although nylon was a big improvement over the
braided silk or linen lines, it is still far from being the
ultimate answer to our fishing needs.
Modern technology has been put to work on ways to
make monofilament lines better for the fisherman.
Advancements in monofilament line seems to be on the
verge of a new frontier, but some of the basic problems
of line strength, kinking, and coiling may never be
solved. It's kind of a give and take situation with some
line features working best for some angling techniques,
but not all. Generally, the smaller the diameter of line
you use, the better fishing you will have, but super thin
lines tangle easily and are relatively stiff. A tough line
for fishing in rocks must be thicker in diameter. A line
that is super limp, which is great for casting, can easily
be broken if the line is only slightly nicked.
The advertising budgets of some of the major line
companies are simply out of this world. This is another
area where I have had a chance to use nearly every major
brand of line on the market. The one guideline

I recommend you follow is that you buy only a "premium quality" line to insure top quality and uniform line thickness throughout the spool. To identify a spool of premium quality line simply look at the outside label for the word "Premium" or "Premium Quality." The extra price you may pay will be well worth it when that trophy walleye is hooked.

CLEAR LINES VS. FLUORESCENT LINES

A long standing debate on the pros and cons of a clear monofilament line for fishing versus the ones with a blue or purple fluorescent property that makes them glow in sunlight is one that may never be answered. The clear line, they say, is more difficult for the fish to see, so you will in turn fool more walleyes. The fluorescent line enables you to "see" the strikes and control the line better out of the water. Which is right? Which is better for you? I would like to say that clear was a better line color, but it has been my personal experience in the last four years which tells me there really isn't a big difference in the final outcome of my angling success. On clear lakes and dirty ones, with live bait or artificial lures, the walleyes NEVER seem to care. Some scientific studies being done indicate that the clear/blue fluorescent lines might actually help attract walleyes!

During a question and answer period at one of my seminars, an older gentleman brought up a fishing trick that I also had used in the Missouri River with fantastic results. He told of a fishing trip when his partner caught six walleyes to his one and the only difference he could tell was that he had been using gold colored line! When the gold colored lines first hit the market, I simply thought they were a sales gimmick for people who have a hard time seeing their lines. This gentleman wanted to know the reason why his partner had been more successful. As it turned out, the lake was a clear one and they had been trolling Rapalas in about ten feet of water. The fluorescent gold line, I reasoned, acted as an attractor for the walleyes who were drawn to strike the Rapala that caught their eye first. This would be similar to the effect of adding a spinner to your live baits to make them look more attractive. When I told the audience this was probably what had happened, the gentleman again stood up and said it confirmed his theory, because when he added a three foot section of gold line just ahead of the Rap, he then caught just as many walleyes as his partner.

Remembering this little trick when I was fishing the Missouri River in North Dakota recently helped to put some very nice fish in the boat. In these waters, spinners are without a doubt one of the most consistently used attractors for walleyes. They are often used with nightcrawlers, leeches or minnows. If a gold colored line could act as an attractor, then this would be the place to see it work. During this trip at least, the gold line used just before my bait DID out-produce the other lines three to one!

I am not proposing that in ALL cases gold colored monofilament line will be the ultimate answer in attracting more fish, but it does prove that bold line colors are not a major excuse for you not to be catching fish and under the right conditions may even improve your catch. It is my firm belief that as long as you have confidence in the color line you are using, it will not hurt your fishing success.

IMPORTANCE OF LINE SIZE

If there is any truth to the statement "the best line is no line," you would then think line size is very critical. Under certain conditions a heavier line is preferred.

While fishing the stump fields of Nelson Lake near Hayward, Wisconsin, I soon learned a walleye in the net is worth six broken lines. The bigger walleyes here love to hide around the root systems of the trees which are found all along the bottom of Nelson Lake because it is actually part of a flowage system that was flooded many years ago. When a large walleye would hit your bait, she would quickly swim back to her home in the roots of a tree. If you didn't use at least twelve pound test, you never saw your hook again.

Anglers, however, SHOULD use the lightest lines they can get by with for several reasons. Smaller diameter lines make your live bait or artificial lures swim and act more life-like. I'm really not a big believer in the theory that if a walleye sees your line he won't strike. The key, I feel, to getting more strikes is to let your bait act as natural as possible. A thin, light and flexible line permits your minnow to swim in a more natural fashion and so appeal to more of those finicky fish. The same holds true when you are fishing with any type of live bait.

Under most circumstances, I recommend four and six pound test lines for live bait rigs, with eight being the heaviest. Many of the commercially made snells come rigged with fifteen or twenty pound test line. Tackle manufacturers must reason that a broken line by an inexperienced angler will result in fewer sales. Therefore, I must recommend that you spend the time it takes to tie your own snells and rigs with lighter lines.

Spinning tackle is obviously the way to handle these light lines, but don't think for a moment that you need four pound test line for your entire spool. Line makers package line in small 20 yard spools called leader wheels to be used just for making leaders that can be attached to a heavier main line. You should attach this leader section with a small #10 swivel, or by tying directly to the main line with a knot called the barrel or blood knot. (See knot tying diagrams.)

The lighter the line you use, the less water resistance you will have. You will also be able to reach the bottom with less line and will need less weight to keep your baits along the bottom. All of these things contribute to a better sense of feel. One thing you will probably notice a lot with light lines is line stretch when you try to set the hooks. There always seems to be a compromise, so make sure the line you use is heavy enough to endure the abuse it will receive wherever you are fishing and yet light enough to allow good natural bait or lure presentation.

It is rather interesting to note that the walleyes in the Missouri River System are seemingly not affected by line size. The reasons for this are really uncertain, but in these special cases you are best off using heavier line to avoid unnecessary loss of tackle or fish!

Fishing Knots

The knot you tie in your line is probably the biggest reason for line breakage. This fact is often clouded over by other excuses, but it's true. The knots you will need to learn will not take you years to master. Basically only two types of knots will cover nearly all your fishing needs for walleye. The BLOOD KNOT is important for connecting two ends of line together and the PALOMAR KNOT for attaching a hook or lure to your line. These are two very important knots to know and practice BEFORE you get into the boat. If you have problems tying the Palomar knot, try the Improved Clinch knot. If you see a special need for any other knots in your fishing, it is important you practice them until you can do them with your eyes closed!

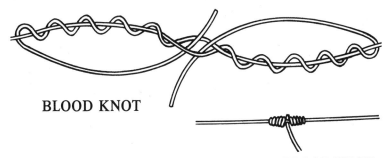

BLOOD KNOT

Want to join two pieces of line together? Use a BLOOD KNOT. When twisting, use five turns on each side, making sure they are in opposite rotations. When the knot is correctly formed as shown, pull it tight and clip off the excess. When the two lines are of radically different diameters simply double-up the lesser diameter line so that there are in effect two lines on one side and then go ahead with the normal procedure. The larger diameter line needs only three twists in the opposite direction instead of the normal five. Some fishermen leave one free end out of the center of the knot as a dropper line and it can extend out as far as 12 inches. Depending on the type of fishing they are doing, a dropper fly can be added or a small split shot attached.

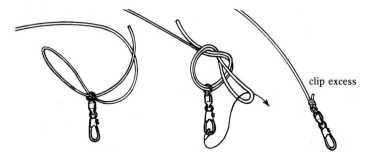

clip excess

The PALOMAR KNOT is considered to be one of the strongest knots known to tie on terminal tackle. The double wrap of mono insures a strong cushion and a strength factor of 85 to 90 percent of the original line strength when tied properly.

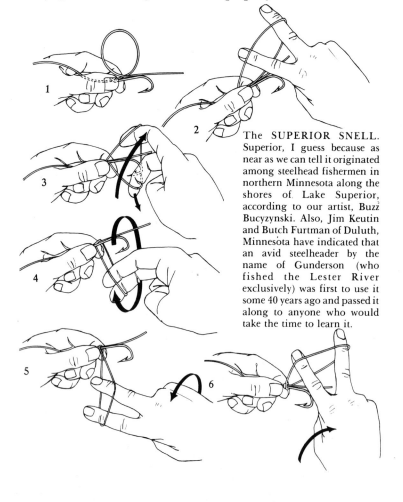

The SUPERIOR SNELL. Superior, I guess because as near as we can tell it originated among steelhead fishermen in northern Minnesota along the shores of Lake Superior, according to our artist, Buzz Bucyzynski. Also, Jim Keutin and Butch Furtman of Duluth, Minnesota have indicated that an avid steelheader by the name of Gunderson (who fished the Lester River exclusively) was first to use it some 40 years ago and passed it along to anyone who would take the time to learn it.

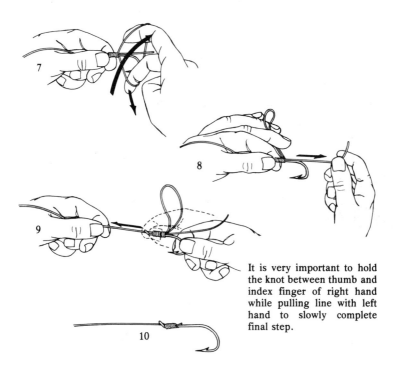

It is very important to hold the knot between thumb and index finger of right hand while pulling line with left hand to slowly complete final step.

HOW TO TIE THE SUPERIOR SNELL

1. With the left thumb and index finger, hold the eye of the hook and form an overhead loop, with a tail extending about an inch and a half.
2. Move the thumb and index finger to trap joining parts of loop. With index and middle fingers of right hand, form shape of loop as shown.
3. Now rotate fingers so that index finger goes over and around backside of hook, while middle finger stays on front side of hook. The idea is to wrap line around shank of hook and extended tail in a symmetrical pattern.
4. The two fingers join together at the bottom of the rotation.
5. Now turn the wrist toward yourself while spreading index and middle fingers outward again.
6. Begin the rotation the same as step 2 and you will notice the line has twisted and wrapped one complete turn on the hook shank.
7. Repeat the step 3 rotation so that you are beginning the next wrap. A minimum total of 7 wraps is needed to make the snell strong. (If you find yourself running out of loop, you can feed more line into it by pulling gently with the middle finger of the right hand on the upward side of step 6.)
8. Trap the final loop between the middle and ring fingers of the left hand and pull the tail with the right hand until you feel it snug up.
9. Now cover the hook and wraps with thumb and index finger of right hand, while pulling the line with left hand until the loop is pulled through. By pulling tail and line until snell is snug, you will insure the knot is completely tight. Slide knot forward to eye.
10. Clip excess tail, and there you have it.

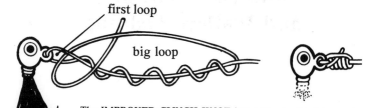

first loop

big loop

The IMPROVED CLINCH KNOT has many applications and can be used to tie almost anything to your monofilament leader. First, run the line through the eye and proceed to make five twists. Pass the free end back through the first loop formed at the eye and then pass it back through the big loop. Pull tight slowly, letting all the spirals tighten uniformly for maximum strength.

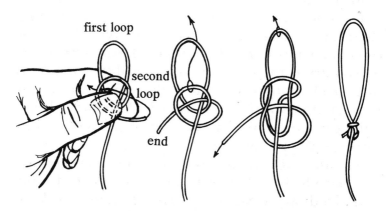

first loop

second loop

end

The LOOP KNOT is used to tie a loop at the end of your monofilament leader when a barrel swivel or snap isn't handy. You will have a variety of uses for this knot once you master the tie. Begin by holding the mono between the thumb and forefinger leaving 4 inches extending upward. With the right hand, form a loop behind the stem and hold the crossing part between the fingers. Form a second loop in front of the first loop again going behind the stem and bring the end around between the two loops as shown. Bring the first loop through the second, pulling slowly upward until the knot closes. You will see where to apply pressure to insure knot forms correctly. As in all knots, do it slowly at first until you master control of the maneuvers.

Modern Electronics and Walleye Fishing

While putting the final facts and subject topics together for this book, a single chapter on the subject of electronic fishing aids did not seem possible. As I organized my thoughts and recommendations, however, they seemed to be condensed into the following major points.

There are many popular names in the field of fishing electronics with Lowrance, Hummingbird or Vexilar common names to many experienced fishermen across the country. Currently there are several different ways to find out electronically how deep the water is under your boat within a fraction of a second. Many of the better units can even give you excellent depth readings at speeds of 50 mph or more!

It's rather difficult to look back twenty years to when fishermen had to use a heavy sinker at the end of a line to find a drop-off. Submerged islands were considered truly virgin waters that only the "old timers" knew about. Today if you were to just spend a few minutes zipping around the lake you would know more about the bottom contours than the old timers who may have fished the lake all their lives! Electronic depth sounding devices can really be a big help in putting more fish in the boat as long as you can take the time to learn what these gadgets can tell you.

The Lowrance "green box" was one of the first sonar

units adapted for the average person to use. Many of the features of the first green box are still used today. The use of a small rotating and flashing bulb is still the best way to understand the bottom signals. This spinning bulb displays electronic impulses that are transmitted through a heavy wire called a coax cable to a hockey puck-shaped device called a transducer. This transducer acts like a microphone and speaker all in one to both send and receive electronic impulses

This portable sonar unit was one of the first available to the general fishing public. This unit was so well designed that many of the originals are still working today!

generated by the main unit. On the rotating dial, a light appears on the zero mark on the dial and again for the depth of water you are in. The distances displayed on the dial are a direct result of the time it takes the signal to reach and bottom and return to the transducer. This can only take place as long as the transducer is submerged in the water or is in direct contact with it.

Transducers come in many different shapes that permit them to work at great speeds. It is EXTREMELY important that the transducer be in direct contact with the water to receive a good signal. The only way it should be mounted in your boat is so you can get a good bottom reading at any speed. The signals emitted by the transducer will vary because manufacturers often give the consumers the choice of selecting a very narrow signal of 9 degrees for an accurate bottom reading in deep water, or a wide angle signal of about 50 degrees which scans a larger bottom area. Although the signal won't be as exact for giving you the depth, it can inform you of nearby drop-offs or even suspended fish. If you are ever given a choice, you will be better off in the long run by selecting the transducer with the widest signal angle available. This wider signal angle is the reason you will be able to better understand what is below the boat while fishing. This may not be an obvious fact right away, but with time you will see a big difference.

These rotating bulb units, or "flashers," are without a doubt the most practical and effective tool for the walleye fisherman. They are called a wide variety of names depending mostly on which part of the country you're from. Flashers, depth finders, fish-locators, fish finder, sounders, or just plain sonar are all nick-names for this important tool.

The rule for running your flasher is to turn it on when you get into the boat and turn it off only when you leave. There is absolutely no reason you shouldn't get a reading at any speed you travel, and you never know when you might stumble onto the honey hole of the century while zipping across the lake. By keeping the "gain" switch on high, it acts like a volume knob that makes sure you will be emitting the most intense signal the unit can produce. By doing this you often get signals that show what type of bottom is below as well as weeds or maybe even fish. Obviously, if the lights start flashing all over the dial and you can't understand what it is trying to say, turn the gain switch down until you can easily see bottom again. If the unit you own or will buy has a special knob for noise suppression to keep out interference from motors or other units, try to keep it as low as possible because this knob will also limit the sensitivity of your original signal.

For a cost of $150 you can purchase an excellent flasher unit capable of recording all the things you will need to know for walleye fishing. Of course, man's ingenuity has led to lots of extra features like night lights, built-in temperature probes, sun visors, swivel mounts, waterproof cases, fish and depth hazard alarms, dual depth scales and the option of having either a portable or permanently mounted unit. Every season manufacturers are striving to add more and more innovations to make them more appealing. Units that show a 0 to 60 foot scale will fit most of your walleyes fishing needs.

The depth of water you are in can also be shown by a straight line of LED lights or maybe even a digital readout. The problem with these kinds of depth finders when compared to the flashers is their inability to give you the extra information a fisherman needs to know about: things like bottom make-up, weeds and fish which are all helpful in putting together the puzzle of catching walleyes. Since manufacturers supply quality instructions on the use and interpretation of their particular product, let me simply recommend you study them closely to learn the full potential of the unit you select.

The most recent major improvement in the fishing electronics industry is called a "graph" or "chart recorder." These units take the same basic principle of the flasher unit, but convert the surges of electricity that would show in lights to burn the signal onto a heat sensitive roll of paper. This type of unit gives a permanent record of depth and other information with amazing clarity. Most graphs have more total signal power than flashers, so they often can tell you some very interesting things about the bottom that a weaker flasher unit may not detect.

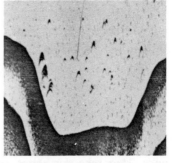

A chart recorder draws the signals onto a piece of paper to make the bottom and the fish easy to see.

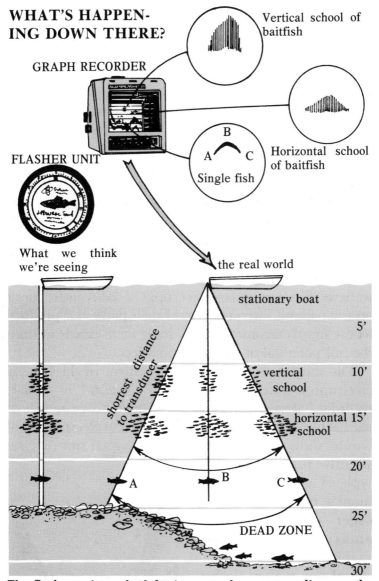

WHAT'S HAPPENING DOWN THERE?

GRAPH RECORDER

Vertical school of baitfish

Horizontal school of baitfish

B
A C
Single fish

FLASHER UNIT

What we think we're seeing

the real world

stationary boat

5'

shortest distance to transducer

vertical school 10'

horizontal 15' school

A B C 20'

DEAD ZONE 25'

30'

The flasher unit on the left gives you the same readings as the chart unit on the right, but in only a one dimensional view for a split second. The graph readings can show individual fish as hooks. They take this shape as the fish come closer to a direct position under the boat and then leave. Note the dead zone in the signal area created by the small ridge along the bottom. This problem is one of the reasons you can catch fish from an area where the graph shows none!

The newest fad in graph units is the use of a thermal printer that uses heat sensitive paper to print the bottom readings. Most graphs on the market today use a carbon treated paper and have a fine piece of wire called a stylus to scratch and burn the paper as it is slowly moved along inside the unit like film in a camera. The carbon paper and stylus system of graph units are by far easier to read and record signals, but the thermal-style printer is usually more trouble free.

If you're looking to invest in a graph recorder, you can expect to pay from $300 to $700. Many of the mounting instructions are the same as for the flasher type units although these graphs are not available in portable models that can be switched easily from boat to boat. The biggest reason for this is that a graph unit will need a much larger amount of power to run in contrast to a flasher unit which can be used for a long time on two six volt lantern-type batteries. A twelve volt wet cell battery is your best source of power for chart recorders.

An even more expensive recorder is the "video sonar unit." An actual video screen is used to display bottom contours and fish signals. The cost here is often restrictive to anyone but the commercial type fisherman at $1,000 or more. It will provide no more information to the angler than the paper type graph units. This little toy does do one thing very well; it reflects the obvious fact that some fishermen will buy ANYTHING!

The million dollar question is, which is the right kind of unit for you? Unfortunately I cannot recommend a single unit for ALL fishermen. However, cost is often in direct relation to the unit's overall performance. One point I would like to stress is that you DO NOT buy a graph type unit until you have mastered a flasher unit first. People seem to believe the myth that the more toys you have, the better the fisherman you must be. Hopefully, this chapter has put these fisherman's gadgets into better perspective. Granted, there are many advantages to using some equipment to make fishing easier and more effective, but these things can only help you to a point. Simply stated, a $1,000 video sonar unit doesn't put fish on your stringer. Once all the sales pitches and sure-fire gimmicks are done, YOU are the person who will still have to catch that walleye!

Where to draw the line on fishing electronics can be a real problem, especially if you subscribe to any number of fishing magazines that are saturated with the advertisements from companies all wanting to out sell each other. Let me advise anyone getting into fishing that it is pure HOGWASH to believe you won't be a good fisherman until you invest $2000 in fishing gadgets. The single most important piece of fishing electronics that you should own would be one of the flasher type units we've already talked about. Stay away from graphs as long as you can, because a flasher unit can tell you nearly everything a graph unit can at a fraction of the cost.

Let me illustrate this point with a little historical fact. In the mid '70's a bill was introduced in the Minnesota legislature to ban the use of graph recorders. The authors of the bill believed that a picture of the bottom and of course, the fish along the bottom would be an unfair advantage to fishermen, and their wide spread use would threaten the state's fish population! What really happened was that the manufacturers had OVER sold the public on what their units could do. A special study was undertaken at that time by the DNR in Minnesota to find out the true effects these units could have on fishing success. Veteran anglers consulted in their report all concluded that using the new graph units didn't help them catch more fish, PLAIN and SIMPLE. The bill never passed!

One last bit of advice—when selecting a new sonar unit: consumers should take the time to study all warranty and service information and EXPECT some problems! No matter who makes the unit or how much you pay for it, you can STILL expect problems. It would be simply foolish for manufacturers to boast that their units are indestructible. Shop and compare well-known product names for cost, features AND warranties.

INSTALLATION TIPS

Be sure to select an area in your boat where you will easily see the units while fishing.

Mounting a trans-ducer should be done so that you can get a good bottom reading at any speed. To do this, mount the transducer near the back drain hole of your boat so that the bottom of the transducer is flush with the hull.

INCORRECT! See how this transducer is mounted and extends lower than the hull. This transducer will create a rooster tail of water when you travel and cause an air pocket to form under the transducer restricting the signal from reaching bottom. You will only be able to get a bottom reading at slow speeds with this kind of installation.

This home-made transducer bracket consists of a short plank of wood and a wood clamp. This practical and inexpensive mounting trick is ideal for portable units and on boats where you don't want to drill holes in the hull. You should be able to get a bottom signal at any speed with this trick. In many cases, this home-made bracket will cost you only a few dollars and be more practical than nearly any commercially made brackets.

Remember the rule, with aluminum the transducers MUST be mounted outside the hull for accurate readings. With fiberglass you can shoot right through the hull. This photo shows how the transducers were siliconed into position to make direct contact with the hull. This will only work in the back drain hole area of the boat where you can reach the portion of the hull in direct contact with the water.

Walleye Fishing Boats

The fishing boats of today's walleye fisherman have changed significantly in the last ten years. Anglers are still searching, however, for the boat which will produce the ultimate combination of class and performance. An avid walleye angler can spend six thousand dollars on the basic boat, motor and trailer combination, without the little frills that can easily add one to two thousand dollars to the total cost of a fishing boat. As walleye fishing increases in popularity, boat manufacturers are really gearing up their boat designs to capitalize on the growing interest in the specialized fishing machine. My advice is to beware of boats "designed by fishermen" because they are mostly designed to CATCH fishermen!

First things first: there is simply no such thing as a perfect fishing boat, car, or house. There may be a boat that is better than another for certain lakes and types of fishing, but let me repeat it again, there is NO perfect boat for all occasions.

This 26 footer is considered the standard walleye boat on Lake Erie.

Again we are faced with a compromising situation. Larger boats are hard to handle, but permit safer fishing on large lakes in rough weather. Aluminum boats are light, but noisy and difficult to maneuver in high winds. On Lake Erie, only boats 18 feet or larger should venture beyond a mile from shore. On small island lakes, a 12 to 15 foot boat can work just fine under most conditions. Deciding which boat is right for you is mostly a personal thing. Anglers interested in fishing waters like Lake Erie exclusively should be thinking of safety FIRST and control second. Ask yourself, "Where will I fish most often? Will I EVER want to spend time fishing some of the larger lakes in my part of the country? What can I afford?" After you've answered these questions, the following information should help you make a wise boat selection that is right for you.

Walleye can be successfully caught from a wide variety of boats. Getting one that's right for you and the water you plan on fishing is very important.

ALUMINUM VS. FIBERGLASS

GOOD POINTS—ALUMINUM These boats are light and durable. They are less expensive than comparable fiberglass boats and have a very high resale value. Their "V" hull designs often handle large waves better than fiberglass designs which are often blunt or lack freeboard above the water.

BAD POINTS — ALUMINUM Aluminum boats float higher in the water and are thus more difficult to control while trolling in even moderate winds. They are often very noisy and may require some extra costs to cover the bottom with a false floor and carpeting.

GOOD POINTS — FIBERGLASS The single big advantage fiberglass boats have over aluminum is that they are far superior for giving the angler better control over the boat at slow speeds for trolling or drifting. In many cases the fiberglass hulls are designed to be more efficient in the water and can travel through the water faster than an aluminum boat of the same size.

BAD POINTS - FIBERGLASS Generally heavier than aluminum, they can prove more difficult to pull behind today's smaller cars and trucks. They are typically designed with modified "V" hulls, so they do not handle the big waves as well. They will cost you more than aluminum and will require more maintenance.

For the type of fishing I do most, I've selected a fiberglass boat, the Ranger 1600. Its new deeper "V" hull design performs well on all but the roughest days. Most importantly, this boat offers exceptionally superior boat control for trolling. The few times I travel to the big waters, common sense dictates if the waves are too much for the boat to handle. Yet a smaller aluminum boat may be the choice for you; it's economical and very easy to control on most lakes. A 14 foot boat with a 25 or 30 h.p. outboard is all that many anglers will ever need.

BELLS AND WHISTLES

Just by visiting a local boat dealer you find that boats of today are not the simple rowboats of yesteryear. Boats with names like "Pro Angler," "Fish Hawk," "Kingfisher" and "Backtroller" are built specifically

These five boats show some commonly used boat designs for
inland waters. The "V" hulls so noticeable on aluminum boats are
a big plus when fishing on those windy days. For smaller lakes or
calmer days, the Ranger 1600 in the top photo can be an excellent
choice in a fiberglass boat.

to meet the needs of fishermen. But remember, the price you pay for a boat will not determine how many fish you catch. Anglers need not feel cheated or threatened by the guy with a $10,000 boat. In all my days on the water I have never yet seen a boat catch a fish.

MOTORS

As with fishing rods and reels where a balanced outfit is important for performance and comfort, the same is true for boats and motors. In many cases the angler may select a powerful motor to get to the hotspots in a hurry, but if you lack the ability to control the boat once you get there, such time saving advantages now become disadvantages!

Selecting the correct outboard for you starts with the type of boat you choose. For safety, comfort and longer engine life, it is best to make the proper motor selection for the boat.

Which motor is best? This is obviously a loaded question that cannot be answered without causing some hard feelings. Anglers should be aware of some performance differences that could affect the decision to buy a particular outboard.

For most 14 foot aluminum boats, a 25, 30 or 35 h.p. outboard will provide excellent performance. If you plan on running three people in the boat for over 50% of your fishing, it would be best to run with the largest motor rated for that boat. Make sure you do not exceed the BIA rating for maximum horsepower which is stamped on a plate near the transom. Most 16 and 17 foot walleye boats are simply too heavy for even a 35 h.p. motor. In this case a 50 h.p. outboard by Mercury or Mariner is your best choice on the market today. This engine has four cylinders instead of two. With the four smaller cylinders, the engine runs more smoothly at slower speeds and you will not foul the plugs or overheat. A two cylinder 35 h.p. motor is far more prone to foul than the four cylinder engines. The 50s with four cylinders have become the most popular choice among experienced walleye fishermen.

When a larger outboard is deemed necessary, you will notice a problem in trying to troll at slower "walleye" speeds. An auxiliary motor of two to ten h.p. called a "kicker" will provide a reasonable solution to the trolling problem. The basic idea here is fine, but actually trolling with this type of arrangement is often not much better than drifting, because you lack the control to stay along steep drops that could be holding all the walleyes.

A small "kicker" outboard is recommended for anglers planning to do some trolling using boats with motors over 50 h.p.

TILLER HANDLE VS. STEERING WHEEL

A "tiller motor" is a motor controlled by an arm directly attached to the motor. It is found on outboards up to 50 h.p. For some reason people have commented that a 50 is too difficult to control by hand, but I personally found them no more difficult to control than my other outboards of 25 and 35 h.p.

Although a steering wheel may provide more comfort when traveling from spot to spot, it soon becomes a disadvantage when trolling. Fishermen will find a big improvement in the way they can control a slow moving boat with a tiller arm in contrast to using a steering wheel. When making a selection for a new motor you may want to pay special attention to the models that have the shifting controls right in the handle as well. This is a big help to make controlling the boat while fishing a one hand operation. Motors with this new feature are becoming very popular with walleye trollers. OMC (Johnson & Evinrude motors) has a shifting arm that can be added to their 25 and 35 h.p. engines to enable easy one hand shifting control. The ability to control speed and direction with one hand is a big plus when trolling. (See photo.) Anglers with a steering wheel must turn and adjust speed with the same hand. Although a friend of mine had mastered the art of controlling the shifting and speed levers with his elbow nearly ten years ago, today he uses a tiller controlled motor.

This shifting arm attachment can make trolling a one hand operation. (available for OMC products only.)

In summary, motors controlled with a tiller handle will give you superior boat control when trolling at slower speeds. This does not mean that if you now own a boat with a steering wheel you cannot troll for walleyes, but it will make trolling more difficult.

PROPELLERS

The importance of using the proper propeller for your boat is far greater than many realize. This is often a big issue for the high speed bass boats, but is often neglected by walleye fishermen. Simply stated, matching the proper "pitch" propeller to the boat's total weight can prolong your outboard's life and increase its performance.

The pitch of a propeller is rated in inches. A 10 inch propeller means that with one complete turn of the propeller, it would be pulling itself through the water 10 inches. The higher the number, the more speed you will get because it grabs a bigger bite of water with every turn. This sounds great if you are looking to increase your total speed, but the higher the pitch is, the less ability the motor will have to push heavy loads. What may be even more important is that you often will not be able to troll down as slowly. The propeller's pitch will vary depending on the size of motor you have. For several years, I guided out of a Lund 315 fiberglass boat with a 25 h.p. motor. This boat was heavy for its size, but my 25 h.p. Johnson was the largest motor this boat was rated to handle. If I ran the boat with just myself, it simply flew with a 12 inch pitch propeller, but when guiding two clients, it would plow through the water like a swimming moose. For these occasions I would change to an 8 inch propeller and the performance difference was like night and day. No longer would my motor labor from trying to push too much weight. Instead, it would put the boat right up on plane. This simple task of changing propellers to a smaller pitch will also permit you to troll at slower speeds and save you money on gas!

OUTBOARD MOTOR MAINTENANCE

The outboard motors of today are much better designed and are far more gas efficient and powerful than the motors of twenty years ago. The proper maintenance of these newer outboards should include regular tune-ups by a factory trained expert. All boat owners should get into the habit of taking their outboards in each fall to have them tuned up and readied for winter. This is one way an expert's eye can see if any major repairs are needed. If you wait until spring, you may find your motor buried with hundreds of others and at this time of year, it may take a month to get it serviced. Regular maintenance that you can do yourself can help avoid many common breakdowns.

Spark plugs are often fouled from excessive trolling or just too much carbon build-up inside the cylinders. By simply replacing or cleaning the plugs you'll notice a big difference in the way your motor starts and runs.

The gear grease in the lower unit near your propeller must be checked monthly. If you notice the lubricant getting milky, water is seeping into the gear case and this could be a sign of a major problem. This lower unit lubricant does wear out and should be changed at least twice during the year. The lube is cheap, lower units are not!

The oil you mix with your gas for your outboard is extremely important to the life of the engine. Use only BIA certified oil. Many discount oils are available at cheap prices, but the end result may be costly repair bills. Whatever brand you choose, take the time to look for the BIA certification!

ELECTRIC TROLLING MOTORS

The modern day walleye fisherman is blessed with many new developments in equipment, and one of the best investments to make your walleye fishing easier and more enjoyable is an electric trolling motor.

The advanced design of today's electronics provides for better performance and efficiency than their predecessors. More often than not, electric motors are a very silent and clean way to troll the "hotspots" of the all too spooky walleyes.

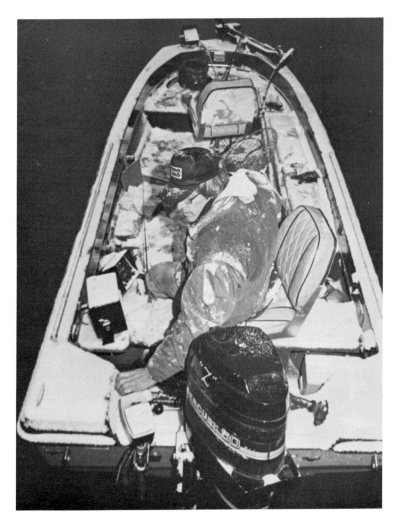

During the cold weather months, an electric motor is often ideal for super slow boat control.

Like an outboard, the electric motors are available in different power ratings, and a balanced match with your boat is important. Most manufacturers provide recommendations in their literature for selecting the proper size motor. The main purpose of an electric motor is to help move your boat about when the conditions are calm. Your gas motor is used when you have some wind. With the more efficient motor designs on the market today, a twelve volt power system is all you will ever need for most fishing boats. A specialized marine battery, however, is very important for supplying enough power to last all day long. The 105 amp deep cycle batteries that cost about $100 are designed for electric motors and the use of anything less may result in a big disappointment. At least a ten amp. battery charger is recommended for giving your battery a full charge overnight. When selecting a battery charger, be sure to get one with an automatic step-down feature or timer built in so it does not boil your battery dry.

A bow-mounted electric motor is a good choice if you plan on doing a lot of casting, but it won't provide good control when trolling because the wind can easily swing the boat into a bad position. A transom mounted motor is the best way for most walleye anglers to go. These lightweight motors are easily clamped to the back of the boat in a position so you can easily reach the handle. The cost of a transom mounted model is considerably less than the bow mounted counterparts.

CUSTOMIZING YOUR BOAT

Without a doubt the best way to avoid the high cost of specialized boats, is to take a standard fishing boat and make it into a fishing machine!

Customizing a lower priced boat will not only save you a ton of money but also will give you a boat that fits your personal fishing needs. Many of the boat modifications shown in this book are not vital to helping you catch more walleyes, but in many cases they will make fishing more enjoyable.

SPLASHGUARDS The basic concept behind splash-

85

guards is to protect the angler from getting soaked as the waves splash against the back of the boat. They also come in hand for keeping big waves from breaking over the transom and swamping you. The technique of trolling backwards is a very effective method of boat control that will be discussed at length in another chapter.

Splashguards test man's ingenuity, and the end result is hundreds of different designs that all work fairly well. The most popular types are removable so you can make on-the-water repairs of your motor more easily and safely. It's a good idea to have the splashguards come up as high as the top of the motor to limit the maximum amount of spray. (See photos.)

These clear splash guards keep the angler dry when the spray from a big wave hits the back of the boat.

Here aluminum was used to raise the height of the transom with a rubber section around the motor for a snug fit.

Removable splash guards are a big plus, because if you ever need to make motor repairs, you have easier access to your motor.

On larger boats the danger of waves coming over the transom is not that great, but to catch the spray that can get you just as wet, you might want to try something like this.

SPLASH WELLS As waves splash over the back of the transom, water that does get through the splashguards gets caught by the splash well and runs back into the lake and not into your boat. If your boat does not already have a built-in splash well, it's a good idea to build one. They can be made of wood covered with fiberglass or a bent sheet of metal that can be riveted into position.

The back portion of this boat was boarded and fiberglassed to create a splashwell to catch whatever water got through the splashguards.

SEATS To fish longer, and more comfortably, well constructed seats are worth their weight in gold. To have padded seats is often considered a luxury by many people, but you will find that fishing walleyes during those slow times can be a lot more enjoyable, and the more time you can spend out on the water, the better your chances become of finding those walleyes.

87

When purchasing a boat seat, try to find the strongest and best made. They will be enduring great stress from the pounding of waves and the rough abuse from the weather. Light-colored boat seats show the dirt more while dark seats get very hot in the sun. The choice is yours.

A comfortable seat makes fishing more enjoyable.

Seat placement is a very important factor that is easy to overlook. The weight of two people on the same side of a boat will cause more spray from the waves and you may needlessly get wet. Proper weight distribution is a very important factor with smaller boats for safety reasons, too. It's best to keep alternating the seats to balance the weight. If you operate the boat from a tiller handle, the offsetting of the seats will permit you to look directly ahead of the boat without having to stretch your neck out of shape. Whenever possible, it is a good idea to keep the other fishermen towards the back of the boat in big waves. This shifting of weight to the back gives a smoother boat ride for everyone and keeps the bow nice and high so the waves won't come rolling over the bow. When trolling backwards into the waves, you will find it is easier to control the boat if you have the other fishermen shift to the front of the boat. This will also help limit the amount of waves that could come over the transom.

FALSE BOTTOM FLOORS Getting around inside your boat need not take the skill of a gymnast. Many aluminum fishing boats are coming out with a flat floor built up above the rounded hull as a standard feature. Raising the floor is a simple task accomplished by cutting a piece of exterior plywood of at least ½ inch thick to the shape of the inside hull. The floor is then supported on the underside with pieces of 2 x 2 or 2 x 4's.

CARPETING Boat floors lined with an indoor outdoor carpeting are not only classy additions to any boat, but practical ones as well. Quality marine carpet wears amazingly well in boats and it obviously increases the boat's total value. By muffling the sound you make in the boat, especially aluminum models, you will scare fewer fish. In the shallows a sudden BANG as you open your tackle box will scare those big walleyes. Carpeting can help solve that problem.

LIVEWELLS In recent years catch and release fishing has been gaining popularity. Anglers are becoming less and less interested in killing what they catch in favor of releasing them to fight again another day. A live well is basically a portable aquarium that can be used to keep the fish alive. The big problem with live wells and walleyes is temperature shock. Although a live well is one of the best ways to hold largemouth bass and keep them alive, the walleye is a much different fish. Walleyes by nature demand a higher percentage of oxygen in the water than a bass. When you put a half dozen walleyes in the same live well they can quickly use up the oxygen unless good quantities of water are added all the time.

A problem even more devastating than lack of oxygen is temperature shock. Often a summertime walleye is taken from deeper, colder depths. As it is quickly brought to the surface, it's body cannot adjust to the rapid temperature change and the fish goes into shock. The surface temperature could be 80 degrees, while at 25 feet it could be only 45 degrees. No matter what you do, the walleye, if you keep it for more than a few minutes, will surely die in a very short time.

Livewells are most effective during the cold water months of the season where the variance in water temperature isn't that great, or the fish are shallow enough not to be affected.

Note the cooler David Hasselberg uses to keep his walleyes alive
as long as possible. Much of the season the cooler is packed with ice
to keep his walleyes fresh.

An old cooler or ice chest can make a great live well
with a few modifications. These portable live wells can
be easily removed at times to make room for more
people. A commercially made live well pump just for
this purpose is often used by bass fishermen and is
available through most marinas for about $35.

Those old coolers actually can serve a dual purpose,
because in the warm summer months you can fill them
with ice and keep the walleyes fresher tasting by
putting them directly on ice as soon as they are caught.

BILGE PUMPS As a boy it was always my task to
get a coffee can and bail out the boat after a rain storm.
It was hard work, and at times when we were fishing, I

couldn't keep up with the downpour. Today this need to physically bail out the boat has been eliminated by the introduction of bilge pumps.

These pumps, mounted in the lowest portion of the boat and powered by the same battery that runs your fish finder, will empty your boat within minutes. A 750 gallon per hour pump is the smallest you should use; be sure to keep the bottom drain area free of debris that could clog the pump.

ELECTRICAL SYSTEM Wiring your boat to run a wide variety of electronic gadgets is probably one of the more challenging projects you will undertake. The actual wiring is really not that time consuming as long as you use common sense and always think safety! Anticipate where problems might occur and work to solve the problem FOREVER and not just for the moment. Look for places to run wires so they are out of the way, dry and free from vibrations which could wear a hole in the wires and cause them to short out. Be sure to fuse EVERY item on the boat to prevent problems from spreading. Be sure to carry an extra supply of fuses of appropriate sizes to replace blown ones. Keep your batteries fully charged and full of water to insure longer life. Keep the terminals clean to avoid any bad connections. There is really no need to skimp on a good power supply because you can never have too much. Again, the 105 amp. marine battery with a deep cycle feature is without a doubt the only battery type you should consider for your boat.

Keep your batteries in a special battery case and attach it firmly to your floor to prevent it from being tipped over. An uncased battery is not approved by the Coast Guard and can damage your boat or clothing with a spill of acid.

When installing switches, make sure they are designed to work when wet. Many times automobile switches are a poor choice in fishing boats because they are exposed to all types of weather and as a result do not last for much more than a season of use.

You may want to take a special look at the commercially made switch and fuse boxes to help organize your electrical system a little better. For operating other electric equipment for short periods of time, like a spot light or radio, you might consider using outdoor receptacals to plug into for power similar to

This Battery Pal serves as a fuse box and battery power indicator in one convenient box. You also have easy access to hook up accessories to the 12 volt system.

what you may have outside your house. These outdoor receptacles wear well in boats and when put in convenient places can really come in handy as a way of getting to your 12 volt system.

LIGHTS U.S. Coast Guard approved lighting is a must for any fishing boat after sunset. A red and green light on the bow as well as a white light in the stern must be lit when you are traveling from spot to spot. When you are still fishing, the white light in the stern must be on at all times to prevent other boaters from running into you. You may want to mount extra lights on the inside of the boat for tying knots at night and one on the outside of the boat for shining over the water to locate your bobber or the shore. A hand held spot is another good item to have along. A popular model called a Q-Beam can really be a help in finding your way back to the boat ramp after dark.

SAFETY EQUIPMENT A horn is another safety device that can come in handy, as well as signal flares, which are now required on Coast Guard patrolled waters, but it is a good idea to have it along no matter where you fish.

A fire extinguisher is something you MAKE room for. Keep it mounted in a place that is easily reached by anyone in the boat.

Life jackets are a must, not only because they are both state and federally required, but because it's good common sense. A walleye is never worth risking your life for, so it doesn't pay to be out on the water unprepared. Be sure to carry an extra flotation device to use to help others if a boat nearby capsizes.

It is not a bad idea to have a CB radio along when fishing remote or extremely large bodies of water. Here, be sure to have the CB tuned to receive the special signal bands used for boats. Your normal car type channels will not receive the boating or "marine" channels. A pocket radio will also keep you abreast of local weather conditions that can affect your willingness to stay out on the water.

GASOLINE VALVE When fishing, the last thing you want to do is to handle an oily gas tank after you go through your first tank. To get around the messy business of changing tanks in rough weather, a tank switching device

Placed in a convenient spot, the angler can easily switch from one gas tank to another.

like those used in trucks is a simple solution. By hooking up both tanks at once you can easily switch from one tank to another.

ANCHOR WINCHES Do you get a sore back or cut hands from pulling up your heavy anchor by hand? An "Anchor Mate" is designed to crank in your anchor and store your rope all in one spot. If you would like, you can also get a bracket made by the same company to hold your anchor near the edge of the boat until you need it again. If you lack storage space and hate to untangle rope, these manual winches are really great. In summary, these customizing suggestions and others that you may discover will provide for easier and more comfortable fishing. Although they may not directly improve your catch, they will likely increase the length of time spent fishing.

Boat Control

Keeping your lure or live bait rig at the proper place and at the proper speed to catch a walleye often takes precise boat control, and trolling is the most popular way to do this.

Getting the bait in front of the walleyes at the correct speed is one of the most important keys to improving your catch. Many anglers are always looking for the secret lure or rig that will produce more walleyes but experience has proven that it's more HOW you fish and not WHAT you are fishing with that often makes the difference. Perhaps the most productive method is to use live bait attached to a plain hook connected to a piece of line about 18 inches away from a weight to keep it near the bottom. This kind of live bait rig is not new or revolutionary, but it does keep the bait down where the walleyes roam most often. Mastering the most effective way to control your boat for the body of water you are fishing is very important to your success. The more methods of boat control you learn, the more consistent you will become at catching walleyes under all types of conditions.

The four methods of boat control we'll be discussing only hit the major categories, but on the water you may need a combination of all of these techniques in order to stay on the walleyes.

TROLLING Very basically, trolling is the act of moving your boat along at a slow speed to keep a lure in a good position for a walleye to hit. This can be done by moving slowly forward or backward while using a gas or electric motor.

Many times walleye anglers pride themselves on stalking walleyes very slowly by trolling backwards. This method is commonly referred to as "backtrolling." By running in reverse, a gas motor will need to run at a higher RPM to push the blunt side of the boat. This will enable you to troll more slowly or even back and forth in a mild chop. Although this

**Backtrolling Along a Point
Sliding With and Against the Wind**

For the most accurate boat control method for trolling, the backtrolling technique is ideal for lakes with steep drop-offs and the times when the walleyes want their bait slow and easy.

method also affords more precise control in the wind, without splash guards an angler will soon find this method of trolling a very wet one! (See chapter on boat customizing.) If you want slow boat speeds on calm water, then an electric motor is a far better choice than any gas engine. The logical use of gas or electric power

These walleyes were all taken from an area no larger than a small car. Pin-point boat control can make a **BIG** difference.

rests mostly with the weather and the speed at which the angler fishes.

On the Missouri River System, forward trolling at almost a jogging pace is most effective in the summer months. For this type of fishing an electric motor is not a practical way to go. If you want to fish with your gas motor, remember that you do not have to always keep the motor in gear. Often by putting the motor into and out of gear you will be able to slow yourself down to a crawling pace if necessary.

Nearly all forms of boat control are dependent on your sonar unit to tell you about the depth of waters below. Without the sonar's help you will have a very difficult time trying to fish areas that are often the best for walleye. It's not that you won't be able to catch some walleyes while trolling without the use of a sonar unit, but you will be spending more time fishing randomly rather than in the "prime" depths.

The ability to hover the boat in one spot takes practice, but can be the difference between limiting out and catching two or three. Walleye schools can easily be packed into groups no larger than a small car. By throwing out a marker buoy, you are able to mark the exact location of the school and fish around it by using a combination of outboard motor power or electric power.

Although trolling is one of the most popular ways to catch walleyes, few learn to master this technique. With the proper trolling methods you will be able to fish in almost any type of water, but especially

A wide variety of marker buoys exist on the market today. If you're not into buying these kinds of markers, you can easily make your own from empty plastic bottles or a piece of hard foam.

in waters with steep or erratic drop-offs where most people cannot fish very well.

Knowing how fast to troll is no simple matter. Every day may require a different speed to produce fish, depending on what kind of mood the fish are in. The rules for boat speed are governed by many factors which fishermen are only now starting to understand. Cold water walleyes (39-45 degrees) often prefer their baits moving slowly. As the water warms, their ability to catch a faster moving bait increases as well.

What is the definition of slow? Slow for walleyes is often to the point of standing still. In fact, at times holding the boat stationary while carefully working an area may be the only "speed" that will produce. The only problem with this snail-like pace of fishing is that is could take you all day to fish a single spot. That is why anglers must become at least versatile enough to use a couple of different trolling speeds in any given day.

FISH LOCATING SPEED   Your goal is to find one overly aggressive walleye in a school to tip you off to the location of the remainder of the school. This speed is often best described as a walking pace. Once a fish or two has been taken from an area, we can now slow our speed down to a crawl and work the bait very slowly to appeal to even the most finicky walleye.

When searching for a walleye school, you should constantly be changing depths as you move in a gradual "S" pattern along a drop-off. At this time, your flasher depth finder is worth its weight in gold. Once the preferred depth has been found, you should stay as close to that depth as possible until you are sure no more fish can be caught there. This is the time where shoreline markings or marker buoys can be a very effective aid in keeping you "on" those walleyes.

Every boat handles differently on the water. This is

one of the reasons practice is so critical to good boat control. Understanding how to best maneuver your own boat under all the different weather conditions is very important.

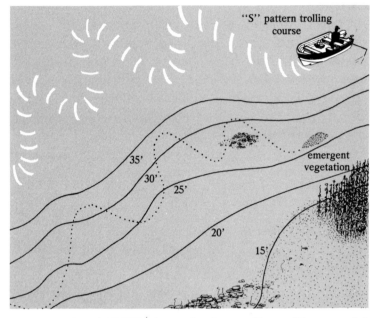

LOCATING WALLEYE As you begin your first trolling pass, it is important to cover a wide spectrum of depths to locate the preferred depth on that day. Once you do locate the walleyes, you should stay at that depth until you no longer catch walleyes.

DRIFTING To many avid walleye anglers, drifting is a big NO-NO! But in some lakes drifting can be both effective and enjoyable. What anglers must understand about drifting is that there is a time and a place for this technique.

If a lake has a bottom shaped like a soup bowl with very gradual drops, this is a drifter's paradise. Many of these lakes are fantastic walleye lakes, too. Lake Erie is a drifters lake without a doubt, with up to 80% of the fish being taken while drifting.

Even though you are at the mercy of the wind, anglers with fiberglass boats drift much slower than a comparable size boat in aluminum. This does not mean you cannot fish productively from an aluminum boat while drifting—you are just prone to be traveling too fast on most windy days.

Drifting randomly through areas with hopes of finding a walleye is probably not much different from making a roll of the dice in a game of chance. It is always a good idea to drift across points or shallow rock reefs whenever possible to increase the chances of your finding walleyes. Shallow fish in particular could be spread out along a shoreline and drifting is a quiet way of getting to them.

Systematic drifting is a good way of checking out a

AREA VOID OF FISH AS BOAT DRIFTS IN

In waters of 12 feet or less, walleyes can be easily spooked as the boat passes over. Note how they will scatter around the boat, but often tend to regroup 50 to 75 feet behind the boat. Anglers can either use a long lining technique or cast in front of or to the sides of the boat as they move along.

lake with a very gradual drop-off. ALWAYS start shallow and work toward deeper water. By placing a marker at the beginning of each drift, you will be able to have a reference point of where to begin another drift.

Once fish are found, it is a good idea to mark the location because you will want to drift through the area again. When this happens DO NOT motor straight back upwind over the fish you will soon hope to catch. Make a wide circle and drift over the undisturbed water. This is especially important when fishing waters of less than 12 feet. If such a precaution is not taken, those walleyes in shallow water will often be spooked by the boat and quickly scatter to the sides. A guideline to follow is that when you are drifting in waters of 12 feet or less, you should let out at least 50 feet of line, or more, in order to get your bait to the walleyes that may be regrouping as your drifting boat passes overhead. (See diagram on page 100). This technique is often called long-lining or flat lining and is especially effective in the early spring.

This nice walleye was taken while the rod was leaning against the side of the boat and permitted to rock back and forth. Many big walleye love this kind of action!

One tip for drifters that can really help their success is to let the boat do the work! To do this all you will need to do is set your rod against the side of the boat and watch the tip. As the wind rocks the boat back and forth, it gives the bait or lure a very tempting action.

A lot of people fish walleyes by drifting. Granted, it is a simple way to move the boat along, but anglers should realize it is not a precise way of finding and staying on tightly schooled walleyes. It's rather easy to get lazy when drifting and even though you might find a school of walleyes, you are often not willing to start the motor and head back up for another pass. Instead, you just continue to drift, hoping to stumble into some more walleyes. Meanwhile, the school of fish you did find begins to move to other areas.

With many boats too large for trolling, drifting can often be the best way to get your bait to a walleye, but

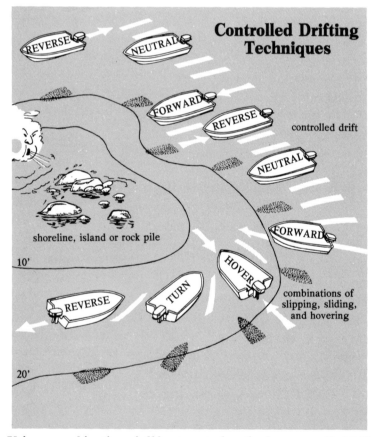

Using a combination of all boat control methods, a controlled drift is a way to follow the shape of a drop-off. The method can be used with either front trolling or backtrolling techniques.

you must realize you are at the mercy of the wind for your direction and speed. That is why drifting is not the most consistent method to produce walleyes in many lakes.

CONTROLLED DRIFT Your ability to keep the boat in productive water is essential. Many times the wind can be used in combination with a gas or electric motor to give you the kind of boat control that can be extremely effective. This technique is the most difficult of all to master, and rightly so. Not only do you need to be aware of the depth, speed and wind direction to control your bait, but you also need to run your motor in an on and off manner to keep your drift going at the speed and the direction you will need in order to catch walleyes. The motor can be used to slow the speed of the drift as well. This slowing of the boat works very well for fishing in big waves. The concept of making a controlled drift is fairly simple, but the actual application of this method varies daily and will demand lots of practice.

ANCHORING Using an anchoring method for catching walleyes may not be the best way of finding walleyes, but once they are found it is the simplest way to cash in on a limit of fish. Trollers and drifters prefer to constantly move about in search of fish instead of sitting in one spot waiting for the fish to come to them. By blending both the searching and catching techniques, you will soon become a more successful walleye fisherman. So, despite the old-fashioned reputation for being a lazy man's way of fishing, anchoring SHOULD be added to your bag of tricks.

The best kind of anchor is either a fork-type or a three-prong mushroom anchor of about fifteen pounds. This weight will hold boats up to 18 feet on most days. At least 100 feet of anchor rope is also needed. It is not that you'll be fishing in 100 feet of water, but the extra length of rope permits you to position the boat well upwind of the walleyes and still allows you enough rope to position the boat within casting range of the school.

When trolling or drifting, be aware of the location of your baits at the time of your strike. The single biggest mistake anglers make when using an anchor is to drop it right on the school of fish. If you were drifting when the first fish hit, you probably went a considerable distance before it was netted, not to mention how much line out you had to start with. If you were fifty feet away, be sure you drop anchor at least 100 feet from the marker you tossed and let out fifty feet of rope to get you

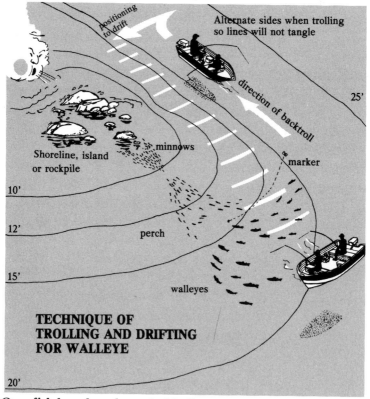

Once fish have been located, this diagram shows how you can drift over the school and then backtroll upwind for another pass. This is the kind of boat control that produces limits!

within casting range of the SCHOOL not the marker!
Another factor critical to your success is knowing
WHEN to drop anchor. The rule to follow is to drift or
troll an area first. Only when MORE THAN one fish
has been taken from a small area is it time to drop an
anchor and work the area over very carefully. If you
randomly drop anchor with the hopes of getting lucky,
your chances of putting a fish in the boat are extremely
poor. A good rule to follow: "Don't wait for the
walleyes to come to you; you must go to the walleyes!"

In high winds DO NOT use a short line to anchor the
boat. You run a very high risk of swamping your boat if
the anchor suddenly catches bottom and holds your
bow down as a wave comes crashing into the boat. By
letting out a long line, the boat is free to ride the waves
better.

JUST THE BEGINNING   The four basic methods
of boat control are very popular indeed, but they are by
no means the only ways to control your boat. At
times it will take a combination of many different
methods in a single day. A walleye fisherman must try
to put himself in the place of the walleye and work hard
at controlling the boat by any means possible in order to
get the bait or lure to the walleye. Speeds must be
changed and depths varied until a preferred method is
found.

Live Bait Fishing

The walleye's diet consists of many different prey, including insects, minnows and small fish. To the fisherman however, this variety is not all that important. In the walleye fisherman's arsenal of attack you will really be working with one of three different types of baits for 95% of your walleyes!! They are minnows, nightcrawlers and leeches. Let's take a look at each of these three and see how they will help your walleye fishing success.

MINNOWS This category of live bait offers a wide variety of choice to the angler. Walleyes will feed on many types of small fish during the year including perch, bullheads, and panfish. Fishermen have basically four minnow types to choose from. They are as follows: SHINERS (Golden or Silver), FATHEADS, REDBELLY DACE, and SUCKER minnows.

Your access to these minnows will vary with the season and the region of the country you're fishing. On some stretches of the Mississippi River, for example, walleyes simply go crazy on a small fish called a Willowcat. It looks just like a baby bullhead and stings like one, too! On the Missouri River System below the Garrison Dam, you can catch walleyes on a dead smelt attached to a plain jig head and dragged along the bottom.

Shiners (Golden or Silver) are a very popular bait throughout the country, but can be very difficult to keep alive. They need fresh water almost constantly and you can never really put more than a dozen in a bucket without overcrowding it. Golden shiners are by far the stronger of the two and are real favorites with walleyes

Shiners

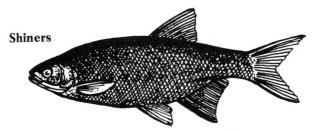

anglers. Shiners are particularly good in lakes with lots of sand. Anglers should try to stay with shiners 1½ to 3 inches long for best success.

Fatheads

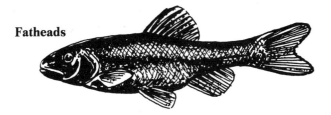

Fatheads are the most widely used walleye minnow in the country. They can be found in bait shops at almost any time of the year. They very seldom exceed three inches in length and are the hardiest of all the minnows. The Fathead minnow, day in and day out is often the best all-around walleye minnow to buy.

Daces

Dace minnows come in many different colors. The Redbelly Dace is becoming a popular minnow with river fishermen. This is a hardy minnow that not only looks attractive with its brightly colored sides, but is attractive to walleyes, too. Some Dace can reach five inches in length, but your best producers will be under three inches.

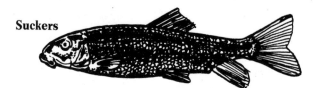

Suckers

The sucker minnow in the right sizes can be deadly on big walleyes. They may be tough to find in some areas, but if you can get suckers under five inches in length, you've got some really great walleye bait. Fall is a prime time to use these small suckers, but the price you will need to pay to get them from bait shops often prevents many anglers from using them regularly.

WHICH SIZE MINNOW IS RIGHT?

The problem of selecting the kind of minnow you use is not really as important as the SIZE of the minnow you select. Spring finds the walleyes in a cold water period and you will be best off to stay with smaller minnows. As the water warms, your minnow size can be increased. The only variation from this theory is during the fall months. By the time fall rolls around, the walleyes have grown accustomed to feeding on larger forms of baitfish, so a large minnow will be very effective.

Minnows in the three inch range or smaller often are more readily acceptable to a walleye and even though a bigger minnow might catch you a bigger fish, your odds of catching a limit are reduced.

HOOKING YOUR MINNOW

There are only a few ways to hook a minnow and it is a good idea to get familiar with the best method for your way of fishing. When casting or trolling, your best off to hook the minnow through the lips. (See photo.)

Place the hook from the bottom lip of the minnow and up. Ideal for casting and trolling because the minnow swims freely and more naturally.

Still fishermen may want a little more wiggle, so you should hook the minnow through the dorsal fin area (as

For still fishing, the dorsal fin area as shown here will be the best hooking location. Be sure you don't place the hook too deeply into the minnow's side.

shown in photo) but be sure you do not place the hook too deep into the body of the minnow becauase it could easily kill him.

When fishing weeds, you may want to try another method using a long shank Aberdeen style hook. The first step is to thread the barb through the gills of the minnow on one side and then pull the hook all the way through the gill plate until you have enough room to place the hook behind the dorsal fin area. The hook will lie along the side of the minnow and if you do not troll or drift too fast, the minnow will do very nicely (see photo). This is also a good method for hooking your minnows when you're fishing walleyes in logs or stumps.

Depending on minnow size, the most popular hook size is a #4 Aberdeen or standard style hook. A

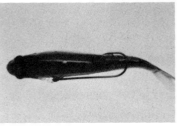

straight eye hook is always the best choice with any live bait. This is a very small but important factor that can increase your odds of getting a better hookset. It is not uncommon to use a #2 or #1 hook for the larger minnows (especially suckers) in the four to five inch range. Using too small a hook with a large minnow is not a very good idea, because it greatly reduces your hooksetting power. As a walleye gulps down your minnow, a small hook could easily be rolled right back into the minnow's body and you will find it very difficult for the hook to hold before the walleye spits it out.

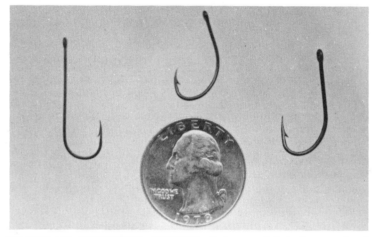

POPULAR MINNOW HOOKS (left to right) Long shank Aberdeen style hook #4, Wide bend Eagle Claw 24R and the standard 84R Eagle Claw both in #4 size.

Adding a minnow to a jig is a very popular combination for catching walleyes. You can either hook the minnow through his lips, or when casting, insert the hook inside his mouth and out his back (see photo) This

This is the ideal way of hooking a minnow if you are doing a lot of casting.

is a very good way of keeping the minnow from falling off the hook.

CARING FOR YOUR MINNOWS

The only good minnow is a fresh lively one. Walleye anglers who plan on fishing with minnows should be extremely aware of their condition. Many bait shops put the minnows into plastic bags filled with pure oxygen. This keeps the minnows alive for hours as long as they are kept cool. Once they leave the bag you must keep fresh water in their container at all times. Do not overcrowd your minnows, especially shiners, If possible, split up your supply into two or more buckets. A flow-through style bucket can

Wendy Koep of the famous Marv Koep's Fishing Pro Shop in Nisswa, Minnesota packs some minnows in oxygen bags for a customer who will be traveling a great distance.

be put right in the water to keep your minnows fresh, but this is a hassle to keep pulling in and out of the water every time you need a fresh minnow. In this case you are best off to store the majority of your minnows in the flow-through bucket while fishing and keep a foam bucket in the boat for holding a few minnows so you will have quicker access to your bait. Foam buckets are far better than metal or plastic because there is better protection from the heat and the foam offers a limited

Minnow buckets come in many sizes and shapes. The price you pay reflects how long you can expect it to last.

amount of oxygen to pass through it.

There is, of course, a wide variety of air pumps available for prolonged trips. This is where an old ice chest with a small battery powered pump works nicely for transporting your minnows long distances.

The colder the water, the less oxygen the minnows will need. A few ice cubes in the water of your bucket will keep them fresher, and in turn they will work harder for you when you are fishing.

NIGHTCRAWLERS This easily found form of live bait is extremely popular for catching walleyes. They are considered the best BIG walleye bait around. Crawlers are said to give off a scent trail that walleyes love. We don't know how true this is, but we do know that walleyes LOVE crawlers!

The time of year for using a crawler varies, but you can expect some fairly decent response from walleyes when the water temperature reaches 65 degrees.

The proper care for

A quality storage container is essential to long crawler life.

your crawlers needs to be one of the most closely watched factors. Within an hour, a whole box of fat juicy nightcrawlers can be reduced to a pile of MUSH! Crawlers are best kept in commercially made bedding material. This material absorbs enough moisture to keep them healthy. It also serves as a great way to keep them cooler. To insure a long and healthy life for your nightcrawlers, you should try to keep them as cool as possible without actually freezing them. In the boat it is a good idea to pack them in a small foam cooler to insulate them from the hot sun. It isn't a bad idea to put some ice cubes in a small baggie and put it right into the box with the crawlers. If you just throw a few ice cubes in the cooler without the plastic bag, you might turn the bedding into a muddy mess. You want to keep the bedding moist, but not overly wet.

Always keep the container out of the direct rays of the sun whenever possible. It may not be warm outside, but the warming rays of sunlight can be a silent killer. Cut or damaged nightcrawlers should be thrown over the side of the boat and NOT into the box with the healthy crawlers. This act will only bring death to your good crawlers if they are kept in that same box for prolonged periods. Between trips, your refrigerator at home is an ideal storage area as long as you do not try to overcrowd the number of crawlers you have in relation to the amount of bedding material you are storing them in.

HOOKING A CRAWLER There are many ways to use a nightcrawler for fishing. One of the most popular is when it is put on a single hook as part of a live bait rig. Here a #4 Aberdeen style hook is a real favorite. Whenever you are using a single hook and trolling, it is best to hook the crawler only once through the thickest part of the crawler's head. If you place the hook farther down the body, you will only get the crawler to roll and twist up you line (see photo).

This is the proper method of hooking a crawler.

Some days you may want to use a crawler harness, especially when you are trolling or drifting at fairly fast speeds or when the fish seem to be extra finicky. A harness often has three hooks and a spinner, but you can make your own very easily with two or even four hooks if you prefer (see knots on page 61). The crawler should be added to these rigs by starting at the head and then putting him on the hooks as they should be placed farther down his body without causing too much of a curl.

Crawler Harness

Note how the crawler is hooked so it will not be needlessly curled. Not hooking a crawler properly could result in line twisting.

Crawlers are often added to jigs to give an extra bit of scent that can persuade a walleye to attack. A crawler used here is simply gobbed onto the hook so it will not be easily pulled off. The same is true for other lures where you would want to add a little bit of extra scent. (see photo).

Adding a crawler to a jig is simply a matter of gobbing it on.

LEECHES The ribbon leech is one of the deadliest walleye catchers ever found. Leeches are effective almost anytime of the year you can buy them. The black or dark brown ribbon leech is found in swamps and is different from its cousin, the common lake leech so many of us see swimming along below the surface. Lake leeches are often larger and very mushy feeling when taken out of the water. They may also have yellow or orange spots along their sides. These leeches for some unknown reason are not as appealing as the ribbon leeches to the walleyes.

The best way to buy leeches is to get them by the pound from your local bait dealer. Buying larger quantities is not only a great way to save money, but you will also be free from the hassle of trying to find bait in some out of the way place. Good quality bait is worth a little extra effort to get and keep. Leeches can be easily kept alive all summer and you don't even have to worry about feeding them. The important thing is that their water be kept cold and clean. It may take a few days or even a week before you notice a white milky film in the water. This is their way of saying it's time to change water. Again a foam box or minnow bucket is the best choice for holding your leeches.

While fishing, you do not need to be as temperature conscious with leeches as you need to be with crawlers. By simply putting fresh lake water into the box every so often, the leeches will do just fine, but DO keep them out of the harmful rays of the sun.

Leeches, like crawlers, can be used by themselves or attached to a jig or spinner for extra appeal. Many walleye anglers prefer leeches over crawlers because they are much tougher and cannot be pulled off the hook as easily.

The most common rig to use with a leech is to put them on a plain #6 hook in either an Aberdeen style or one of the wide bend type hooks as shown in the photo.

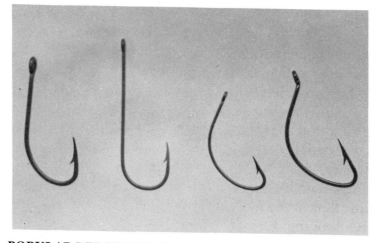

POPULAR LEECH AND CRAWLER HOOKS (left to right) 84R Eagle Claw 36, Aberdeen style hook #6, Kahle Hook #12, and Mustad Hook 37160 #8.

When hooking a leech, you must first consider how you plan on fishing. When still fishing or trolling at a very slow pace, you will want to hook the leech from the bottom up near its big sucker end. This will make the leech swim away from the hook and also serve as a strong place to put the hook. On the other hand, if you are moving along at a rather rapid rate, you will be better off by hooking the leech through its head or NON-sucker end. This will prevent the leech from balling up as you move, and present the leech in a natural manner. You see, the non-sucker end of the leech is his head, and leeches swim HEAD FIRST. The

Hooking a leech through the sucker end is best for still fishing.

vast majority of the time you will be hooking a leech through his big sucker end, but if you notice it coming back all rolled into a ball, you may want to try hooking him in the head.

In many mid-western locations, leeches are sold in

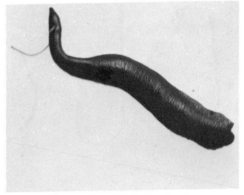

Hooking a leech through the NON-sucker end is best for trolling or drifting at faster speeds.

three popular walleye sizes: medium, large and jumbo. Everyone has his own definition of a jumbo leech, so the sizes you buy will vary considerably. Day in and day out the large size of leech will end up being about three inches long when stretched out. This size will be the most consistent no matter what time of year. If you can get some really jumbo leeches in the fall, they should prove to be a great bait for BIG walleyes.

These are the three major types of live baits walleye anglers can use and are most often found in local bait shops. There are, of course, a few forms of bait that can work on special occasions. These include frogs, salamanders, water dogs (immature salamanders), Hellgrammites and crayfish. These forms of live bait and others that may be used regionally can be extremely effective for walleyes. The big drawback with these baits is that they are often difficult to find and the walleye's interest in feeding on them may be very short-lived.

Walleyes can often be caught using waterdogs, which are immature salamanders.

Popular Live Bait Rigs

A sinker attached to your line and then a piece of line from the sinker to the hook dressed with some kind of live bait is a simple definition of a live bait rig. The diagram shown on the following page gives examples of some of the more popular commercially made rigs. Many walleye lovers prefer to make their own rigs to help keep the cost of fishing down. Looking at an expert walleye angler's tackle box, you might not be too impressed. The basic sinker and hook combination is the bread and butter equipment for many avid anglers.

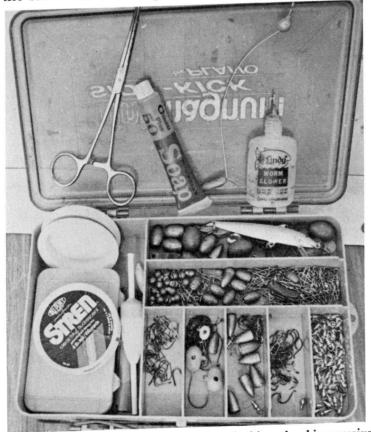

A tackle box of a walleye expert need not be big to land impressive catches.

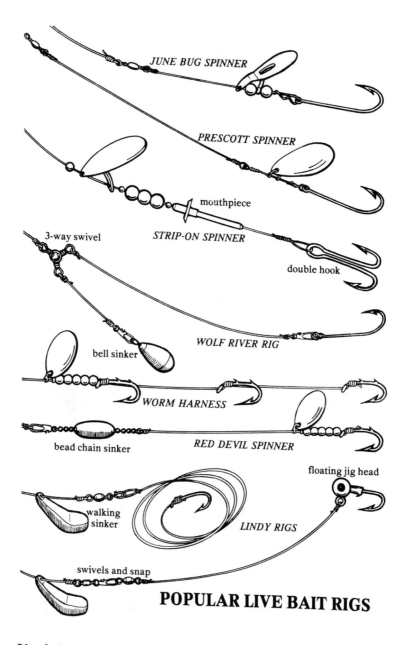

JUNE BUG SPINNER

PRESCOTT SPINNER

mouthpiece

3-way swivel

STRIP-ON SPINNER

double hook

WOLF RIVER RIG

bell sinker

WORM HARNESS

bead chain sinker

RED DEVIL SPINNER

floating jig head

walking
sinker

LINDY RIGS

swivels and snap

POPULAR LIVE BAIT RIGS

Live bait rigs come in many different designs.

ATTRACTOR SNELLS In many lakes, competition for food is not a big problem. Walleyes here can be difficult to catch because everywhere they turn there's a free meal. The high abundance of baitfish can turn a lake with a very high population of walleyes into a lake that seems simply void of fish. By adding an attractor of some sort to your bait offering, you can often get those walleyes to strike. The goal here is to make the bait different from anything else they might see.

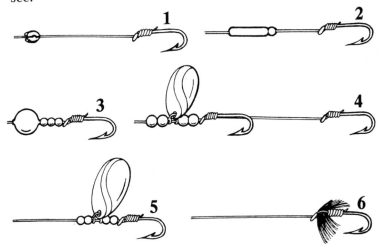

1. A plain snell (such as the SUPERIOR SNELL) with a single split shot works in the weeds and casts well. The split shot is often 12 inches from the hook.
2. There are adjustable floating heads on the market that can be threaded on your line quickly. They control how far off the bottom your bait can be whether drifting or trolling. (Lindy-Little Joe)
3. Corky floats are a favorite with many walleye fishermen. They also are threaded on the line. A few beads just ahead of the hook give the clearance needed for good hook setting capabilities. (Northland)
4. A double snelled spinner rig will allow you to set the hooks as soon as a strike is felt.
5. A spinner rig popular for walleye in Canadian lakes and the Missouri River System.
6. The YARN RIG is a SUPERIOR SNELL laid back on the hook shank. The proper color yarn is inserted between the snell and the eye of the hook, then pulled tight. Trim the yarn as you see fit. Remember, the yarn does give the rig a degree of "lift" in the water and some fishermen claim a walleye has more difficulty in spitting out the yarn because it can get caught in his teeth.

This little trick of using attractors could range from simply using a small orange bead in a very clear lake to a big spinner in a dirty lake. Many anglers believe it could be the motive of competition that gets the lazy walleye excited. Seeing a minnow struggle with a piece of orange ball may fool the walleye into thinking he'll never get a better chance at a quick meal and he'll gulp it right down before it's too late.

Whatever the reason for their effectiveness, live bait rigs with a spinner, bead or float are definitely popular among walleye fishermen. It is often a good idea to have each member of the party fishing with a different rig until a preferred system is found for catching them that particular day. The walleye's preference for one color or type of rig can change at any time. Walleyes can also get bored with seeing only one color. You may hit a school of walleyes and without any problems take six nice fish. Suddenly the fish turn and you can't catch a thing. Now is the time to switch from the yellow spinner rig you were using to a red one or some other color. This is sometimes all it will take to start catching walleyes again! This is especially true when you are fishing walleyes that are confined to a very small area.

FLOATING JIG HEADS A ball of hard foam attached to a jig hook may look as if it would sink, but this small foam ball serves as an effective attractor and a way to keep your hook suspended above the bottom when it is appropriate.

Hooking a minnow on a floating jig head is best done by going from the bottom lip through the top. Some floating jigs have the eye where you tie your line pointed inward toward the barb. Under slow speeds the minnow will struggle to right itself because the hook will want to be pulled downward so the eye faces the bottom. To get around any twisting problems you may have from trolling at higher speeds, simply hook the minnow through his eyes.

The better types of floating jig hooks will have the eye either turned away from the barb or have the eye in a straight line with the shaft of the hook. These two types of hooks will give you better hooking power and reduce line twist. A #4 hook works well for leeches and crawlers, and a #4 or #2 works well for minnows depending on their size. The color of the floating jig you select is a personal thing, but chartreuse (bright yellow/green), fluorescent orange and white have proven to be the most effective for me.

There is a wide variety of float/attractors you can put ahead of your bait. Here are a few you may want to try: (top to bottom)
Northland, Float 'n Cork Rig
Quality Tackle, Glow-Go
Worth, Walleye Wackers
Windels, Walleye Snacks
Mister Twister, Floating Jig Head
Phelps Floater
Gapen, Baitwalker Floating Jig

SPINNERS A colored spinner attached just in front of the hook is often a popular way to get the attention of the walleye. The size of spinner you select is often changed with the season. During spring and fall the walleyes will tend to prefer a smaller spinner. This may be due to the clearer waters found at these times of year. Summer walleyes like the bigger size spinners. A #4 or #3 size in an Indiana shape blade is a popular size in the commercially made snells available in most tackle shops. A spinner also can keep your bait just above the bottom if you are trolling at a rapid rate. The parachute effect of the spinning blade can often be used when you have a need to keep the bait just above the bottom. Popular colors are silver, gold, orange and yellow. To get the full benefit of what a spinner can do, you are best advised to use them at times when you are traveling fast enough to make the blade spin.

SINKERS Anglers must consider very carefully the size sinker they use when setting up their live bait rigs. Keeping your baits near the bottom is very important, and unless you take the time to select the kind of sinker to best get you down to the bottom, all of your later efforts may be wasted.

Depth and speed are the two major factors you must consider when selecting a sinker weight. Please take note of the following chart:

Split shot	1 to 3 feet
1/16 ounce	3 to 8 feet
1/8 ounce	8 to 12 feet
1/4 ounce	12 to 15 feet
3/8 ounce	15 to 20 feet
1/2 ounce	20 to 25 feet
5/8 ounce	25 to 30 feet
3/4 ounce	30 to 35 feet
1 ounce	35 to 40 feet

With this chart it is important to realize that on windy days you will need to go to a heavier size sinker and the same is true if you are using a very heavy line. Water resistance often increases in these two conditions and it will be much more difficult to stay on the bottom unless you use a heavier weight.

There are many different shapes of sinkers on the market that all do something different. The importance of a specialty shaped sinker is really far less important than most would have you believe. The bell-shaped sinkers are some of the most practical on the market today. The Water Gremlin Company sells selections of sinkers with a fast clip feature so you can simply clip on or off the sinker size of your choice. The more expensive bead chain sinkers are really great for faster trolling, but if you are fishing in or near snags, this kind of sinker can make fishing rather expensive. Walking type sinkers are designed mostly for live bait fishing. They are often expensive and impossible to change sizes without retying. These "sliding sinkers," as they are often called, were made for a special way of fishing. I'll be talking about that very soon.

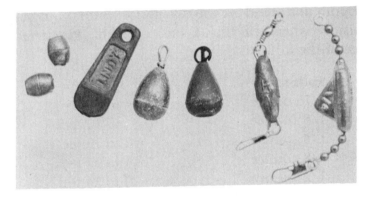

Popular sinkers for walleye fishing (left to right) Water Gremlin Egg Sinkers, Lindy Walking Sinker, Water Gremlin Fast Clip Sinker, Snap Swivel Trolling Sinker and Bead Chain Keel Lead.

Snag-less sinkers all claim to be the perfect answer to fishing in areas with lots of lure-stealing snags. In the following diagram we show several of the more popular models. You often do not have the variety of weights to choose from, but under the right conditions you will find these types of sinkers CAN save you a certain amount of time and money.

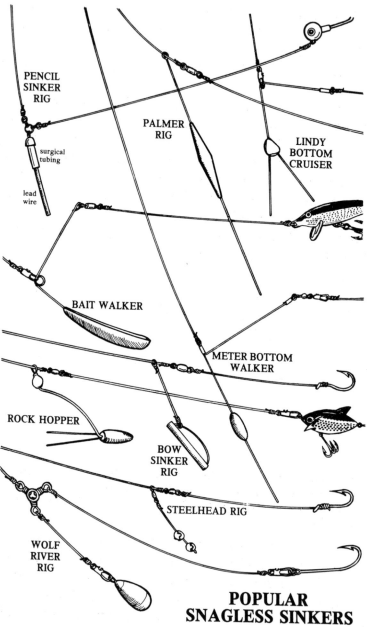

PENCIL
SINKER
RIG

surgical
tubing

lead
wire

PALMER
RIG

LINDY
BOTTOM
CRUISER

BAIT WALKER

METER BOTTOM
WALKER

ROCK HOPPER

BOW
SINKER
RIG

STEELHEAD RIG

WOLF
RIVER
RIG

**POPULAR
SNAGLESS SINKERS**

Any serious walleye fisherman makes sure a good selection of sinker sizes is always in the boat. You never know when you may need to change to a different size or shape sinker.

SWIVELS Swivels protect your line from being twisted and serve as a device to stop your sliding or clip-on type sinker from sliding all the way down to the hook. Swivels are commonly used in the making of live bait rigs because they connect the snell to the rest of the line. If you plan on using four pound test for a snell and ten pound test on your fishing reel, then I do advise the use of swivels to connect the two different lengths of line. Swivel size #8 and #10 are very popular for this purpose.

A small split shot works just great for stopping your sliding sinkers at a fraction of the cost, and with a substantial savings of time. One important problem that must be considered is that if you pinch the split shot onto the line too tightly, you could be weakening the line. This is one easy way to set up a live bait rig with a snell length that can easily be changed.

SNELL LENGTH When working with a live bait rig, one of the most important factors to consider is the length of snell you plan to use. Changing the distances the hook can be from the sinker can have a great effect on your success and your ability to fish certain areas. The rhyme and reasons for using long snells really comes down to a trial and error system. To start out, on most fishing trips, you will begin fishing with a snell about 18 inches long. On lakes that are very clear, it is a good idea to never use a snell UNDER three feet in length. In dirty water lakes you will be better off to keep your snells shorter. It is not all that uncommon to be fishing with a snell only one foot long under very dirty water conditions. The thing that you, the fisherman, have to remember is that you have got to get the bait to the fish no matter how long or short a snell you use. If they are holding tight to the bottom, shorten up your snell. If the water is very clear (as I have mentioned), the walleyes may suspend above the bottom a few feet, so anything you can do to get the bait off the bottom and up to the fish can be helpful.

This is all leading us to the age old question, "How will I know where the walleyes are?" The answer is a very obvious, YOU DON'T! I certainly would like to come up with a system for telling you where the walleyes will always be in relation to the bottom, but it is just not possible. The only way to really know is to take the time to check it out yourself! By starting with a snell 18 inches in length you will be at a good length to shorten or lengthen as needed. If possible, use the other members of your fishing party to try other combinations because this can really make a difference in the total outcome of the day. It really is not as bleak as it sounds, because 80% of the walleyes you will be catching will be coming from within the first two feet above the bottom anyway.

FISHING WITH A LIVE BAIT RIG

Without a doubt, live bait rigs catch the greatest number of walleyes. Understanding how to adapt this basic rig to your particular fishing needs may require much trial and error, but let's look at some of the most commonly used applications.

PITCHIN' This term describes the method perfectly. You use a small split shot about 18 inches up the line from the hook and pitch it out from your boat. This method is often used in shallow rocky areas where snagging may only take seconds with a heavier sinker. You can effectively fish this method by drifting slowly or anchoring. With such a light sinker, it obviously must be fished very slowly and for best results you shouldn't be fishing any deeper than 10 feet.

LONG LINING One of the most popular methods of fishing live bait rigs is long lining. Many people do not really understand just how effective this method can be under certain conditions. Often called flat lining, this method is deadly on walleyes in 12 feet of water or LESS. Let out 50 to 75 feet of line so your live bait rig is kept away from the boat. This will eliminate spooking the fish.

When I was a youngster growing up, our family owned a large run-about boat with a big outboard motor. My father never wanted to troll, so we would drift instead. At that time I had no idea what long lining meant. By habit I would let out great amounts of line to keep the bait as far from the boat as possible. At that time there probably wasn't a fancy term for this method of fishing, but it worked just fine for me.

Later, I began to understand that in shallow water, the large boat would spook the walleyes to the side, but if enough line were let out, the walleyes had time to regroup behind the boat.

While fishing with this long lining method, it is very difficult to "feel" anything. At times you may not even know if your bait is on the bottom. This is another reason why this method should be used in shallow water only. In most cases, if you are not drifting too fast, a few splitshot are enough to keep the bait near the bottom without dragging in the weeds or muck. Since your sinker and hook will be 50 to 75 feet away, it is wise to reel in and check it periodically to make sure weeds and other debris have not gathered around the bait.

Maybe this technique for walleye fishing is TOO simple, but it is VERY effective!

The single biggest problem with this method is one of hooksetting power. You have so much slack line out at the time of a strike it is very difficult to set the hooks properly. Anglers fishing with this long lining method are sharply reminded NOT to give the fish any slack line once you feel a strike. With all the slack line you already have out, it is to your advantage to simply drop your rod tip to the fish and when the line grows very tight, pull straight upwards as hard as you can. Using this technique of live bait fishing, it is impossible to set the hook too hard!

The hook sizes I have already recommended for the different kinds of live bait should be followed for this and all live bait fishing methods, but for this long lining method, one hook style in particular has a definite advantage. The fine wire Aberdeen style hooks have a very fine point that will pentrate the tough mouth of a walleye much easier than a standard hook. The finer hook point can make the difference in catching a walleye at long range.

Sinker size is often not more than ⅛ ounce unless you are drifting or trolling very fast, when a ¼ ounce sinker may be necessary to get you to the bottom. Another factor that may play a part in your sinker

Long lining is a simple but effective trick that anyone can master. These early season walleye were taken in only a few feet of water using the long lining method for the first time.

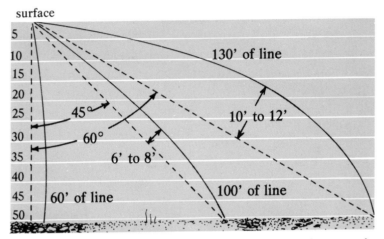

selection is the size of line you choose. A thicker, bigger diameter line increases water resistance and will act like a parachute for your sinker and bait in the water.

LINE BOW CREATED BY WATER RESISTANCE

The resistance put on the line while pulled through the water is something we have little control over.

In early spring when the walleyes are often in only ten feet of water or less, a bobber can be used in the same fashion most people fish for crappies. This long lining technique can work very well with a bobber and has some advantages over using just a plain line. If, for example, you are drifting through a shallow rocky area, the usual sinker and hook combination will snag in a matter of seconds. A bobber will suspend your sinker and bait just above the rocks and be in perfect position to catch your fish.

LINDY RIG METHOD One of the most popular sliding sinker rigs in recent years was developed by Ron and Al Lindner of Brainerd, Minnesota. Learning to use this method of live bait fishing begins with knowing how a walleye strikes your bait.

Contrary to what people may have heard, the walleye when it feeds is not a nibbling fish—it's a gulper! If a

132

walleye did indeed go around grabbing the tails off the minnows, he sure wouldn't eat much! When a walleye big enough to keep attacks your bait, he will hit it head first and in a gulping fashion! A predator fish like the walleye prefers to attack forms of bait that he can swallow with one gulp. If your bait returns to you all chewed up, then you must do a little adjusting if you want to start appealing to the remainder of the school. Some days when a walleye puts a death lock on his prey it may not be swallowed down his throat, so you can

either give the walleye enough time to swallow the bait down completely, or simply use a smaller form of live bait! A hit from a "keeper" fish is often very different than one from a small fish. But, on rare occasions, the big walleye could be biting like a small fish with a series of short little tugs. This is more

Anglers of all ages can master the Lindy sliding sinker method to catch walleyes of all sizes.

unique than typical walleye feeding and striking habits.

Now that we know a walleye is an effective predator fish, the Lindy Rig method still needs some more background information before we can put all the pieces together. You see, as the walleye swallows your bait offering with a gulp, you often will not feel that powerful strike on the other end of the rod, even though you have just spent $200 on the most expensive rod on the market. It is a problem with all live bait fishing methods EXCESS LINE! Not only do you have large amounts of slack line in the water due to the uncontrollable water resistance factor, you also have a line stretch problem. The distance of line you are using from your sinker to your hook is another source of slack line that can contribute to your inability to feel the strike.

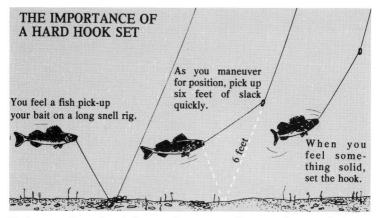

THE IMPORTANCE OF A HARD HOOK SET

You feel a fish pick-up your bait on a long snell rig.

As you maneuver for position, pick up six feet of slack quickly.

6 feet

When you feel something solid, set the hook.

Understanding what is happening as a walleye grabs your bait is a part of getting a good hookset.

When you're long lining, at first you might think you have run into a weed instead of a walleye, but the only way you will find out which is which is by simply doing nothing! If you continue to drag that weed and it does not show any signs of life, then it is a weed. If it continues to come steadily with you and starts to tug back, then you have yourself a walleye! They feel the same almost every time, and although you might not feel a spectacular strike when the walleye grabs your bait, it still can be a nice fish. To review the hooksetting technique for long lining once more, you simply point the rod tip to the fish, wait until the line gets tight and then pull the rod straight up with all the strength you can muster. It is not uncommon to wait a total of ten seconds after the fish is first felt before you strike.

134

The Lindy Rig excels when you're fishing directly under the boat in waters of 12 feet or more. You are fishing with a much shorter line at this time, but a strike may still be felt as a sudden increase in the weight of your sinker. If you are feeling a series of rapid taps you have found perch or panfish. A walleye, when he strikes, tends to have much more weight behind the tugs.

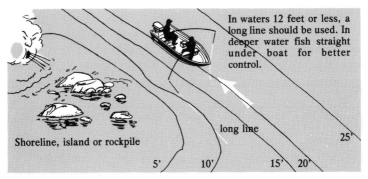

In waters 12 feet or less, a long line should be used. In deeper water fish straight under boat for better control.

long line

25'

Shoreline, island or rockpile

5' 10' 15' 20'

While long lining in shallow water a walleye might feel a lot like a weed. In deeper water fish with a short line straight under the boat. A walleye strike will be much more aggressive or simply feel like a sudden increase in the weight of the sinker.

Now with the Lindy Rig method of using a sliding sinker, you can feed line to the walleye after he strikes. By just the nature of the colder environment the walleye lives in when you are fishing in deeper water, the walleye's reflexes are often slowed to a point that you will need to give the walleye time to get the bait all the way into his mouth. This is simply done by letting the line flow freely off your reel whenever a strike is felt. This actually helps with more than just giving the walleye enough time to swallow the bait. In long lining you need to wait before you set the hook because you really want to know if you hooked a weed or a fish. The other reason you waited is often not considered. By waiting before you strike, you will be getting a better angle for a hookset! If you would set the hook as soon as any resistance is felt, the hook would have a hard time finding a place to hold as long as the fish was still facing the boat. By giving the walleye several seconds to turn downward or sideways, you have just increased your odds of a better hookset. So with a Lindy Rig, you will be feeding line to the fish to help give yourself a better angle of hookset and also to give the fish time to swallow the bait completely.

When you're giving line to a walleye with a sliding sinker rig, the length of time you let the fish "run" should begin with only five or six seconds of free line. If you are still having problems getting the hooks into the walleye, then increase the amount of time given before you set the hook until you find out how aggressive the fish are. The procedure for setting the hooks with a Lindy Rig is to re-engage the reel once you have given the fish some time to run with the bait, take up as much of the slack line as you can and try to RIP HIS LIPS OFF! Ideally you will want to stay as close to the striking fish as possible to reduce the amount of extra line you may have out before you strike. This means you may want to put your motor into neutral while you're feeding line to the walleye.

Long rods really can pay off big for live bait anglers. A six to seven foot rod is very typical for live bait fishing with the long lining method. The sweep of a long rod can take up the extra slack line that could be the difference between a good hookset and a poor one. A POOR HOOKSET IS PROBABLY THE BIGGEST REASON FOR MISSING A WALLEYE.

SLIDING BOBBER RIGS The logic in our fishing has never been more obvious than when you start talking about using sliding bobbers to catch walleyes.

The actual use of bobbers is kid's stuff, right? WRONG! This newly rediscovered rig for walleye fishing is one of the most deadly live bait rigs ever devised! The real beauty of this rig is that anyone can master it.

If you're having problems fishing in rock infested areas or stump fields, your problems are over! Another one of the advantages with this system is that you can fish for walleyes at any depth with a bobber. The logic in using a bobber begins when you start having problems trying to stay away from all the lure-eating rocks or debris along the bottom. "If you can't fish productively from the bottom up, why not fish from the top down?" This sounds so simple you would think everyone would be doing it. In some regions of the country however, this method of fishing has NEVER been tried.

The newly refined slip bobber rig has won many a walleye tournament in recent years, but some experts simply refuse to use bobbers because they are just TOO EASY! Indeed, the art of bobber fishing could be mastered in only a few minutes to provide first time anglers with the kind of success others just dream about. Being able to suspend that bait right above the bottom in front of the walleye is something that can often take years of practice. Even a newcomer to bobber fishing can really clean up! In some regions of Minnesota for example, guides would love to see bobber fishing banned on some of the better walleye lakes! That is just a little indication of how deadly they can be.

The actual operation of a sliding bobber rig is nothing new, but by looking at the diagram, you can see that most of the components have been designed for lighter weight monofilament lines. The hollow tube in the bobber permits even the lightest of lines to run through it without causing any problems. The line is stopped at the desired depth by using a bobber stop. They come in a wide variety of sizes and types and are

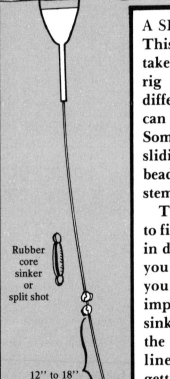

bead

slip
bobber

Quik Stop Mfg.

Arnold Mfg.

Fin Mfg.

Bobberstops

Rubber
core
sinker
or
split shot

12'' to 18''

leech

A SLIDING BOBBER RIG:

This diagram shows what it takes to make a sliding bobber rig work. There are many different kinds of bobbers that can be used for this type of rig. Some, made especially for the sliding bobber rig, have a small bead already inserted into the stem of the bobber.

The depth you are planning to fish will be the biggest factor in determining the bobber size you should use. The deeper you plan to fish, the more important it is to have enough sinker weight. This will enable the weight to quickly pull the line through the bobber, getting the bait to the depth you need. Make sure the bobber is held just under the halfway point, where it will give the least amount of resistance to a walleye swimming away with the bait.

available at most tackle shops. It is important to place enough sinkers on the line to keep the bobber you select floating straight up and just over the halfway mark. This will permit the least amount of resistance for the walleye when he pulls it under. Place the sinkers about 18 inches above the hook so your bait is free to swim about.

The real tough part about catching walleyes with a sliding bobber rig is knowing WHERE to fish. Basically, bobber fishing is best suited for fishermen who anchor. If you are anchored in the right spot, get the landing net ready. Anchor in the wrong spot and you might as well take a nap.

The easiest thing to do to find walleyes on a popular walleye lake is to simply follow the other boats! This is obviously a good time to have a pair of binoculars in the boat. The other choice you have is to drift or troll an area until a school is found, then simply drop anchor well upwind of the school and bobber fish by casting back to them. If you're spending more than a half hour in one spot without results, MOVE! Don't get lazy!! Remember, you never want to wait for the walleyes to come to you, you must go to the walleyes.

Leeches are the number one bait among bobber experts with a Fathead minnow a far second. When still fishing, be sure to hook the leech through the sucker end for best results.

When setting the hook with a bobber rig, it is difficult to know exactly how long a fish has had the bait. This is why so many fish are gut hooked when caught with bobber rigs. Small, non-keeper size fish enjoy the tasty meal you supply all too well, and end up gut hooked. When you do run into a school of small hungry walleye, it's best not to rip their guts out just to get back a 5¢ hook; instead, cut the line near the hook and retie. The walleye can easily discharge the hook in a few weeks. A

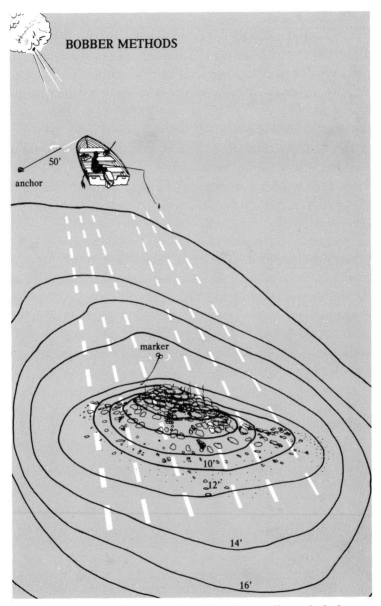

BOBBER METHODS

50'

anchor

marker

10'

12'

14'

16'

This diagram shows how you should anchor well upwind of a possible hotspot and let out enough anchor rope so you can cast onto the area you wish to fish without spooking the walleyes.

walleye is simply too valuable to waste needlessly!

Now once a walleye has grabbed the bait, watch the direction the bobber travels. As with the other live bait methods, a good walleye will have your bait swallowed in only a few seconds. It is a good idea to wait until the bobber is moving AWAY from you before the hooks are set to give yourself a much better hook setting angle. It is again important to stress one last time that the slack in your line will dampen your hookset unless you take up as much slack as possible BEFORE you set the hook.

Artificial Lures

Although many anglers simply do not believe a walleye can be caught on artificial lures, there is a time and a place where they can be very effective. Knowing WHEN to use an artificial lure is probably just as important as where it is fished. Adding the use of artificial lures to your arsenal of attack will only make you a better angler.

One basic rule in walleye fishing that is the cornerstone of success for the artificial bait fisherman is: "Shallow water walleyes are aggressive walleyes." These are the fish that can be caught with artificial lures. The guideline to follow is that when-ever you find walleyes in ten feet of water or LESS they can be caught with artificial lures. In water DEEPER than ten feet, live bait is a much better choice.

Shallow water walleyes can easily be caught on artificial lures.

Now that we know the depths where an artificial lure can be most effective, let's take a look at the type that will give you the best results.

PLUGS This type of artificial lure has really gone through some changes with the discovery of new plastics and foams. In the old days a plug was carved from a piece of wood to resemble a minnow. The plugs have a new name now and a much newer look. The modern-day walleye angler doesn't fish a plug anymore, they now call them crankbaits. This new term has helped anglers rediscover how effective the old time plugs are.

Crankbaits: Here are a few of the baits often used by bass fishermen which are very effective for walleyes as well: (left to right) Normark Fat Rap, Mann's Deep Pig, Rebel Deep Wee R, Bagley's Small Fry, and Bomber Model A.

When a popular walleye lure called the Rapala first hit the market, they were so effective that bait shops would rent them out for $25 a day! It is surprising how lures this effective can become passing fads. Twenty years ago Rapalas, Lazy Ikes and Flatfish were the most deadly things going for walleye fishing. Even anglers who didn't have any of the fancy depth finding devices so popular today caught plenty of walleyes. The real question is will these old fashioned methods for catching walleye still work today? YOU BET!!!

Back in their heyday, plugs were used along shorelines simply because there was no way of knowing how deep the water might be in the other areas farther away from shore. With the introduction of the flasher type depth finder, a whole new experience awaited the walleye fisherman. The new found ability to fish in deeper areas for walleyes caught on like wildfire. This soon found the older methods of walleye fishing falling off in popularity in favor of the "scientific" approach of fishing deeper water walleyes with live bait rigs.

The popular Rapala at the top of this photo brought a whole new meaning to the word "plug." Others on the market today that are also popular [left to right] L & S Mirr-O-Lure, Rebel Jointed minnow, PH Wabbler, Cotton Red-Fin Minnow, and Lindy Baitfish

The big hush-hush secret among many walleye experts today is the rediscovery of all those super shallow walleyes that were easily caught by anglers of yesteryear. With a better understanding of lure and boat control in shallow water, these walleyes can offer fantastic fishing!

Night is often considered a prime time for fishing with artificials because the walleyes tend to move into the shallows when feeding. One point that must be stressed, however, is that walleyes can be found shallow all day! This fact may surprise many anglers who believe that all the walleyes in a lake consistently move to the shallows from the deep water areas on a lake. This may be true in some cases, but one thing you can rely on is that some walleyes will ALWAYS stay shallow no matter what the time of day or type of weather conditions that develop.

In chapter 1, some very important facts about walleyes

144

were covered. Three things that control where a walleye can live are FOOD, SECURITY and COMFORT. Some lakes have more potential for keeping walleyes in the shallows, but in any given lake, river or reservoir at least, some of the resident walleyes will be in the shallow waters of ten feet or less where crankbaits can effectively be used to catch them.

When selecting crankbaits, make sure you get a few different types that are designed to run at different depths. Remember, you will always want to stay very close to the bottom, and lighter lines

The old fashioned "plugs" are still a great way to outfox walleye.

of four to eight pound test will help make it easier for the crankbaits to reach the bottom. The faster you crank in your lure the SHALLOWER it will run. Many people think if they crank fast the bait will dive deeper,

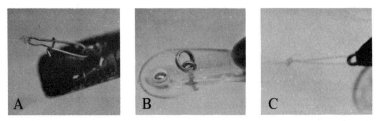

To get the best action out of your crankbaits, it's best to attach the line in some way so the lure is free to wobble; (A) Shows a plain snap, (B) "O" Ring, (C) Loop Knot.

but what really happens is that your crankbait looses its ability to dig and as your water resistance increases with speed, the downward pulling ability of the lure stays the same. The end result is a crankbait running a full foot or two shallower than it could under ideal speeds.

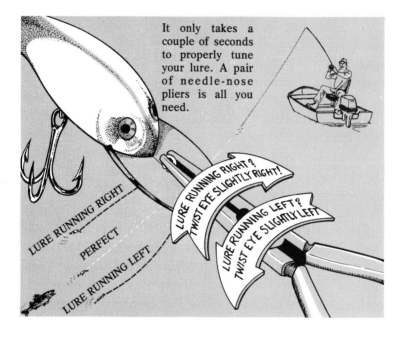

It only takes a couple of seconds to properly tune your lure. A pair of needle-nose pliers is all you need.

A commonly asked question is whether or not the new photo-print finishes common with many of the newer crankbaits actually look more realistic to the walleye. To date, nothing proves that these realistic looking baits are more effective than conventional colors, but fishermen are sure to bite on them!

JIGS: This traditional walleye lure is one of the most widely used lures in the world. Simply put, a jig is a hook with a piece of lead attached to its shank. The size and shape of the lead will permit the jig to be fished in a wide variety of places.

When jigs first became popular with the walleye fisherman, the hook was dressed with chicken feathers or deer hair. By shaking the rod tip, a jig could be danced in the water in a very appealing way and the walleyes just loved it. Today anglers can find jigs in every tackle shop in the country. They come in almost any size and color. Some are made with rubber bodies and tinsel instead of hair or feathers.

Jigs today come in many different shapes and are made with a wide variety of materials.

The reason I think jigs are so consistently effective is that they stay near the bottom. You don't need to be an expert in order to catch fish with them, just keep them as close to the bottom as you can and you have a very good chance of catching a walleye with one. Depending on the depth of water, jig size should vary. (see chart)

1/16 ounce	1 to 3 feet
1/8 ounce	4 to 8 feet
1/4 ounce	9 to 12 feet
3/8 ounce	13 to 16 feet
1/2 ounce	17 to 22 feet
5/8 ounce	23 to 28 feet
3/4 ounce	29 to 34 feet
1 ounce	35 to 40 feet

As with sinkers, the size jig you select could be one or

maybe even two weights heavier if you are in the wind, current, or using a heavy line.

When jigs were first developed, they were used with great success just with a few feathers or a clump of deer hair, but today it's common to "dress" the jig with live bait. By adding a minnow to a colorful jig, you will make the combination look a lot bigger in the water. Early spring walleyes will often prefer a smaller bait fished slowly near the bottom. To make your jig and minnow combination look more "bite size" it may be wise to remove some of the feathers or better yet, use just a plain jig head with a minnow added.

Fishing with a plain jig head is often kept a secret among avid anglers. A plain jig head and minnow can often be the answer for catching those

Many experts say jigs are the #1 big walleye bait on the market today!

finicky walleyes. You can also add a piece of nightcrawler to your jigs to make them more appealing. There is no big trick here, simply gob it on the hook so it won't fall off when casting. Leeches can also be used on a jig by simply attaching the leech through his sucker end only once and let him trail out.

The shape of the jig head also affects its action. A round headed jig is very popular for fishing straight under the boat. A wedge shaped head or "stand-up"

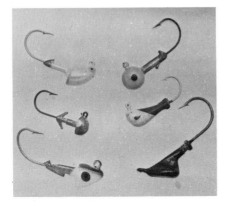

The shape of the jig head will give you different actions in the water.

head like those found on the Lund Backswimmer jigs work very well for casting because once it hits the bottom, the hook still points upwards at an angle a walleye can easily scoop up. Anglers are reminded to tie your line directly to the jig for best jig control and action.

JIG FISHING TECHNIQUES Although it is easy to learn the basics of jig fishing, there is a special art to fishing a jig that can take years of experience to develop.

Other books may stress the importance of the "proper" technique for jig fishing, but there is no such technique! THERE IS SIMPLY NO RIGHT OR WRONG WAY TO FISH A JIG! The beauty of fishing with jigs is that they can be used in a wide variety of ways. The only guidelines I can suggest are the following:

1. ALWAYS KEEP A TIGHT LINE
2. KEEP YOUR JIG NEAR THE BOTTOM
3. SET THE HOOKS QUICKLY

Three basic, yet productive actions you can give to your jig is (1) let it drag the bottom (2) hop it along the bottom and (3) swim it just above the bottom.

All three of these fishing methods are popular and all have their moments, but it's very important for anglers to realize that a walleye's preference for one technique is never consistent. In the morning they may want their jigs hopped, but by noon they may want them simply dragged along the bottom. Trial and error is all part of the walleye fishing game.

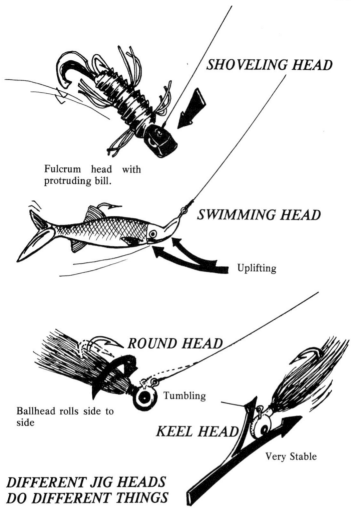

SHOVELING HEAD

Fulcrum head with protruding bill.

SWIMMING HEAD

Uplifting

ROUND HEAD

Tumbling

Ballhead rolls side to side

KEEL HEAD

Very Stable

DIFFERENT JIG HEADS
DO DIFFERENT THINGS

When selecting the type of jig shape to buy, keep in mind how you intend to use it. The round and keel headed shapes are best for fishing under the boat and the shoveling or swimming head shapes are best for casting.

Color selection is often down-played because most experts do not want to stick their necks out. Predicting the best color for all occasions is impossible, so I would like to suggest a few effective ones to start you out. Since fluorescent orange is the most visible color to the walleye's eye, it must rate as one of the top colors. The

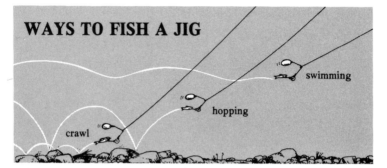

WAYS TO FISH A JIG

swimming

hopping

crawl

There is no right or wrong way to fish a jig, but here are three popular actions walleye often LOVE.

Jig with trailer hook.

Be sure to insert the treble hook into the minnow.

In snags or areas of moss, insert the hook in the top of the dorsal fin [as shown].

other would be chartreuse (bright yellow/green), black, yellow and white. In my opinion, one of the most under-rated colors for walleyes is BLUE! Of course, at times color may not make a bit of difference, but when staring at a wall of a hundred different colored jigs at the local tackle shop, this advice should get you going.

When your retrieved jig and minnow combo has teeth marks on it or is half eaten, you probably are being hassled by a small fish. Only on rare occasions will you find big fish biting so finickily. A common problem when this happens is that the jig you are using is just too large for the walleyes to handle. A trailer hook is a small #8 or #10 treble hook attached to a very short piece of monofilament line, and the other end is tied directly to your main hook. (See photos on previous page.) Once your minnow has been added, simply insert one of the treble hook barbs into the bottom side of the minnow. In an area with lots of snags or moss, you should insert the treble in the top side of the minnow's back.

Different Waters
Different Techniques

This major chapter on how to fish various types of walleye water found around the country is intended to illustrate major factors or special techniques that will make you a more versatile and successful walleye fisherman.

In previous chapters you read about boat control methods, how to balance your equipment and how to set the hook on a walleye. These basic principles hold true for fishing all over the country. One of the hardest things for anglers in different regions of the country is to accept the fact that a walleye is a walleye, no matter where it lives. How it survives may change from lake to lake, but it is still a walleye and while its behavior may be influenced by varying habitats, the basics remain unchanged.

Up to now you have been shown the "bread and butter" methods for catching a walleye. This should serve as an excellent base of information to improve your success no matter where you fish. But now let's look at specific places and areas that are very popular among walleye fishermen to see how they have modified some of these basic methods to increase their success.

WALLEYES IN RIVERS

Walleye in rivers are basically shallow water fish. Only during the extremely cold seasons will a walleye be found with an consistency in water OVER 12 feet! River walleye show a big preference for rock shorelines or rock covered bottoms where the current slackens. Sand areas are their second choice and when walleyes are found in sand, they are often there to feed. Muck bottomed areas on a river are the least attractive to a river walleye.

Two primary factors a "river rat" should be concerned about are CURRENT & BOTTOM. Simply stated, current breaks make it possible for the walleye to relax and by keeping your bait on the bottom, you greatly increase the odds of putting the bait right in front of the walleye. Suspended walleyes, in rivers just do NOT exist!

Moving water tends to counter the effects of a cold front, so when a severe cold front system moves through your area and simply shuts down all lake fishing activity, you are better off fishing a river.

Dams serve as excellent holding areas for river walleye. This is especially true on older rivers where most of the shoreline is sand or muck. The obvious

Catching big walleyes in rivers means you need to keep your bait tight to the bottom at all times.

current breaks made by the dam itself are very visible and if you can find wing dams nearby, you are definitely in great walleye water. A wing dam is a pile of rocks and logs that can come in many different shapes. They are placed in the river by the Army Corps of Engineers to increase the river's speed and to prevent sediment from filling in the main channel and restricting boat navigation. These rock piles are best fished by anchoring (see diagram on next page). The points of these wing dams, like points on a lake, have the greatest

154

Dams form a natural holding area for walleyes and are a prime area to fish in the spring and fall.

potential for holding walleyes first. Some wing dams are very long and stretch almost completely across the river channel. Here the big walleyes are not behind the wing dams where the largest current break is found, but just in front of it! Larger walleyes prefer to station themselves on the UPSTREAM side of the wing dam. This small section of dead water in front of the wing dam permits more baitfish to be swept right in front of their noses!

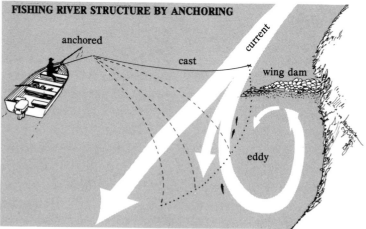

FISHING RIVER STRUCTURE BY ANCHORING

anchored

current

cast

wing dam

eddy

As a wing dam creates an area of dead water for the walleyes to get away from the current, anglers are best off to fish these areas by anchoring in the river's main current to hold them in position long enough to find the walleyes.

Although anchoring is generally preferred when fish are located or you want to fish a specific spot, you may want to backtroll into the current to hold the boat so you can fish an area for a brief period. You can also easily make the boat slide parallel with the current to fish the entire area in front of a long wing dam similar to the one I have described. It is not all that unusual to

Wing dams and other current breaks are ideal for walleyes to hold behind. Note the dead water area created by this pile of rocks. Walleyes will love to feed near areas like this.

use a one ounce sinker in only ten feet of water if the current is swift. A river walleye will not travel very far to grab your bait, so you must keep it as close to him as is possible, and that means, ON THE BOTTOM!

Jigs are the number one river lure and it may not be necessary to add live bait because the walleyes often don't have time to see what is swimming past. They grab first, think later! It may be a good policy, however, to add live bait to your jigs when the conditions are tough, just for extra insurance.

The live bait rig is popular, and short snells are recommended. The Wolf River rig is a popular choice with river anglers because with a lighter weight dropper line holding your sinker, you will often be able to break off and save the rest of the rig when badly snagged.

Another important guideline to remember: walleyes ALWAYS face UPSTREAM. For consistent catches, you should be working your baits by casting them upstream and bringing them downstream right in front of the walleye's nose. This is true for trolling as well.

You want to work across or downstream with your baits so that the walleye is more prone to see and grab it. On the other hand, a walleye sitting downstream from you is looking straight at you. Many times the hook will be

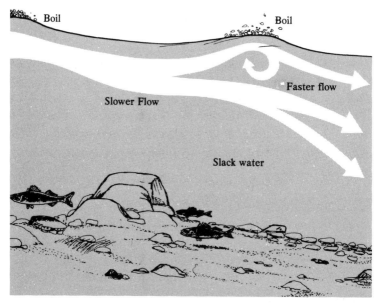

Boil

Boil

Faster flow

Slower Flow

Slack water

In rivers, walleyes can find life very comfortable behind a rock or any other kind of current obstruction. Note how the boil is downstream from the actual rock. Remember, if you want to get your bait in front of the walleye, you must "lead" the boil by fishing well upstream.

pulled right back out of his mouth when he does grab your bait. The angle of the hookset has never been more important! When you are forced to fish downstream, it is better to wait a second or two before you set the hooks so the walleye will have time to drop back to the bottom or return to the rocks he was hiding behind.

Being more aggressive than their lake counterparts, river walleyes are often taken on crankbaits either trolled or cast. For shallow rocky or sandy areas, shallow running crankbaits are an excellent choice.

They can be most effectively used when cast upstream or across stream and retrieved at a speed that will give them good action.

Trolling with jigs or live bait rigs is done WITH the current. Ideally you will want to float downstream slightly faster than the surface current speed so you will have a better feel of a strike. An obvious change of technique from lake fishing to rivers is that you want to keep your bait straight under the boat at all times when you are in eight feet or more of water. The spooking problem in lakes is not nearly as important in rivers. It will be to your advantage to stay on top of your baits for two very good reasons. You'll have better depth control and feel, and it will lessen the chances of being snagged on the bottom.

Another popular and effective technique for catching river walleyes is to use a vertical jigging bait. Some of the more popular lures are the Heddon Sonar and the Cotton Cordell Gay Blade. By quickly snapping your rod tip up and down, you can often excite the walleye to grab these thin pieces of metal that will easily get to the bottom in even the strongest current.

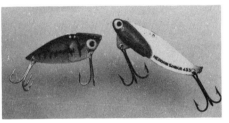

The Gay Blade (left) and the Heddon Sonar are just two very effective vertical jigging lures for rivers.

The walleye often hits the bait just before it falls to the bottom and when you snap the rod tip back up for the second time, you are in essence setting the hook. Many times you can foul hook a walleye with this lure because the treble hooks are openly exposed to snag anything that comes near it. Many anglers refuse to use them for exactly that reason. The ½ ounce sizes are the most widely used and a small snap is recommended to attach the lure to your line. You know when the bait is working well if you can feel a strong vibration every time you pull upwards.

BACKTROLLING THE JIG

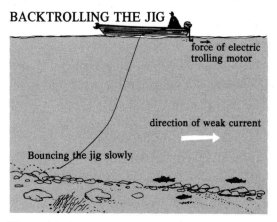

force of electric trolling motor

direction of weak current

Bouncing the jig slowly

When trolling with the current, it is best if you can move your boat slightly faster than the speed of the current so you can feel the strike more easily.

CHANGING WATER LEVELS   Since all of our rivers rise and fall several times in a season, it is best to know how these changes in water levels affect angling success.

A stable water level is without a doubt the ideal condition. Although fishing can be super in high or low water conditions, a stable water level will permit walleyes to set up a consistent feeding pattern.

A gradually rising river is also a good sign, but floating debris can make fishing more of a challenge. Rising water means the walleyes will move shallow to cash in on the heavy feeding activity of the minnows and crayfish that feast on the insects found along the newly covered river banks.

A falling river level is the worst condition. Fish can sense a decline in water levels, no matter how small and quickly shift to deeper water. It may not be a bad idea to head to a lake when you know the water levels are dropping!

SEASONAL LOCATIONS DNR studies have shown that river system walleyes can migrate 200 miles in the spring to reach spawning areas. They can often be found just below a dam, spillway or major rapids. When spawning is completed, walleyes will slip back downstream and take up positions along rocky rip-rap, near wing dams or sandy bars. Summer walleyes really do not move around much and you can expect to find them in the same areas for the whole summer season.

In the fall, walleyes often experience a feeling of spring and some begin a kind of false spawning run. Again, dams, spillways or the base of a major series of rapids is where they will group. Although many sportsmen would prefer deer hunting in the late fall, the chance of catching a trophy river walleye is never better. In most areas you will have the river all to yourself, too.

Can you tell the difference? The fish on the top is the Sauger, the walleye's look-alike cousin commonly found in rivers. Sauger often have the black spots along the dorsal fin and their bodies have black or gray splotches. A sauger likes deep, dirty water in contrast to the walleye, and it never gets as large.

RESERVOIRS

What is the true definition of a reservoir? Webster defines it as "an artificial lake where water is collected and kept in quantity."

These man-made bodies of water today hold some of the finest walleye fishing in the country! The next world record walleye is surely to come from one of the many southern reservoirs so popular for their largemouth bass fishing. These southern reservoirs are nearly untouched for walleye because many anglers in this part of the country are not even aware that walleye exist! Locals catching a walleye often bring them in to bait shops to have someone identify the strange looking fish. Many readily admit that no one knows how to fish for them, so nobody bothers!

Fishing a reservoir is really not much different than fishing a lake and in many cases, it's easier.

Since many reservoirs are flooded river systems, walleyes in them are apt to travel great distances. When we talk about a reservoir, there are basically two different kinds: a highland reservoir, which is often rocky and very deep, and the lowland reservoir, which is mostly flooded trees and bottomland. Where the walleye can find spawning areas will control where they will move to in the spring. In a highland type reservoir, walleyes may travel great distances upstream in many cases to get to the shallow spawning areas. In a lowland type reservoir, walleyes are victims of tough conditions and in many cases a shortage of necessary spawning sites. Walleyes will then be forced to roam DOWNSTREAM if that is where they can find spawning areas. Flooded road beds or old gravel pits, along with the banks of the shore near the dam itself, can be used by the walleyes if they need to.

In either a highland or lowland reservoir, there are a

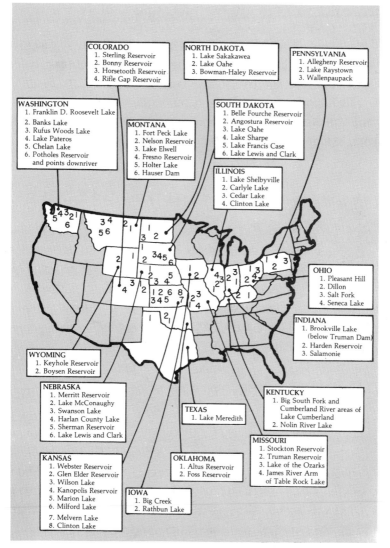

COLORADO
1. Sterling Reservoir
2. Bonny Reservoir
3. Horsetooth Reservoir
4. Rifle Gap Reservoir

NORTH DAKOTA
1. Lake Sakakawea
2. Lake Oahe
3. Bowman-Haley Reservoir

PENNSYLVANIA
1. Allegheny Reservoir
2. Lake Raystown
3. Wallenpaupack

WASHINGTON
1. Franklin D. Roosevelt Lake
2. Banks Lake
3. Rufus Woods Lake
4. Lake Pateros
5. Chelan Lake
6. Potholes Reservoir
and points downriver

MONTANA
1. Fort Peck Lake
2. Nelson Reservoir
3. Lake Elwell
4. Fresno Reservoir
5. Holter Lake
6. Hauser Dam

SOUTH DAKOTA
1. Belle Fourche Reservoir
2. Angostura Reservoir
3. Lake Oahe
4. Lake Sharpe
5. Lake Francis Case
6. Lake Lewis and Clark

ILLINOIS
1. Lake Shelbyville
2. Carlyle Lake
3. Cedar Lake
4. Clinton Lake

OHIO
1. Pleasant Hill
2. Dillon
3. Salt Fork
4. Seneca Lake

INDIANA
1. Brookville Lake
(below Truman Dam)
2. Harden Reservoir
3. Salamonie

WYOMING
1. Keyhole Reservoir
2. Boysen Reservoir

NEBRASKA
1. Merritt Reservoir
2. Lake McConaughy
3. Swanson Lake
4. Harlan County Lake
5. Sherman Reservoir
6. Lake Lewis and Clark

TEXAS
1. Lake Meredith

KENTUCKY
1. Big South Fork and
Cumberland River areas of
Lake Cumberland
2. Nolin River Lake

MISSOURI
1. Stockton Reservoir
2. Truman Reservoir
3. Lake of the Ozarks
4. James River Arm
of Table Rock Lake

KANSAS
1. Webster Reservoir
2. Glen Elder Reservoir
3. Wilson Lake
4. Kanopolis Reservoir
5. Marion Lake
6. Milford Lake
7. Melvern Lake
8. Clinton Lake

OKLAHOMA
1. Altus Reservoir
2. Foss Reservoir

IOWA
1. Big Creek
2. Rathbun Lake

WALLEYE RESERVOIRS: Walleyes can be found in reservoirs all across the country. Some of the largest walleyes in the United States come from these man-made lakes. For more detailed information on each area, contact the state's fisheries department.

few rules you can apply in locating walleyes:
1. Look for wave action or current.
2. Stay in waters of less than 15 feet.
3. Fish shoreline points near deep areas.
4. Fish very close to the bottom.

Highland reservoirs are often lined with steep breaks, and as long as you are able to stay at a depth the walleyes like, you will do just fine.

WALLEYE DO LOVE TREES!

Walleye in many lowland reservoirs will adjust to a new life style of living in trees with no problems at all!

In lowland reservoirs, walleyes live in a different world. They still need FOOD, SECURITY and COMFORT, but these walleyes find it by hiding near old tree stumps! Bobber rigs, weedless hooks and sinkers are very popular among stump fishermen. Many of the flowage lakes in Wisconsin are full of tree-loving walleyes. Without adjusting, traditional methods of fishing would simpy frustrate anglers with constant snags. The edge of an old river channel where is passes close to these stumps can be the real prime waters for walleyes.

Rigging up for heavy timber conditions

Clip lower hook

cut

cut

Customizing your baits for certain conditions is an important part of staying flexible with the methods you use for catching walleye no matter where you fish. By removing the bottom treble hook, a Rapala can be fished without snagging as easily.

THE MISSOURI RIVER SYSTEM

One of the world's truly great walleye waters is the Missouri River System flowing through North and South Dakota. A series of four large reservoirs has been formed by dams to help control flooding and supply electrical power to the midwest. This walleye fishery produces well when you use a combination of river AND highland reservoir methods. The abundance of three to six pound fish from these waters may leave you with the impression that the walleyes are less intelligent than their lake counterparts, but I believe the walleyes are just plain more vicious!

Smelt is the major food source in this system and it didn't take long for the walleyes here to realize that by packing together in large schools they could stalk the swarms of smelt with great success. As a result, they have become a highly competitive fish, learning that aggressiveness means survival!

Hotspots on the vast Missouri River System are really not too difficult to find. The problem is that when you look at a map, you soon become puzzled about where to start. The temptation is to travel great distances to reach areas other anglers might mention, but my experiences have taught me that by starting near the boat launch, you can save a ton of money on gas and catch just as many fish.

The walleyes in these waters spend a great deal of their time feeding in deep water. This is a very difficult time for anglers because both the smelt and the walleyes move about constantly. By looking for deep water near an obvious shoreline point you will often have a great place to start. The walleyes often move to the nearest point of land and hold there between feeding binges. Newcomers to the area are often told by local experts that it isn't necessary to fish until 11 a.m.! The smelt chasing walleyes move to the nearest point next to their feeding areas and often stay there until 4 p.m.

Wave action pounding the Missouri's soft clay banks often creates a white milky band of water near shore. Walleyes often move into this discolored area to feed. Not all the walleyes like to chase smelt—some prefer to move into the shallows and feed on minnows and perch.

Lunch time walleye fishing is often the best action of the day on the Missouri River.

Spinner rigs are very popular in these waters especially when used with a nightcrawler. During the summer months this spinner and crawler rig is without a doubt your best bet. A jig and minnow combination is tops in the spring and again late in the fall.

Seasonal movements of walleyes are noticed by anglers, but probably the most noticeable differences occur in June. On Lake Oahe in South Dakota, the walleyes will often be biting like crazy on night-crawlers, while on Lake Sakakawea in North Dakota anglers can't buy a fish! Farther north the water is much cooler and the walleyes just take a little longer to become aggressive. Here the walleye fishing really doesn't turn on until July. On a recent trip to North Dakota during a cool spring, the locals reported that fishing was poor on the big lake. By adjusting my angling techniques as though it were early spring, I had no problem finding and catching walleyes. The first thing I did was use a plain white jig and minnow combination. The lake had not thermoclined as yet which meant the temperatures and oxygen levels were the same all the way to the bottom. This also meant the walleyes were free to roam to any depth. That day all the fish came from thirty feet of water or more! When the water begins to warm, you very seldom fish any deeper than twelve feet.

Although the methods of fishing with live bait or artificials are really no different than the methods already written about in this book, it may be interesting to note that anglers here often use 20 pound test line and heavy bait casting rods! The walleyes here simply don't care how heavy a line you use. It's impossible to tell how long this kind of fishing will go on, but one thing is for sure, it's some of the finest walleye fishing in the world!

If you are planning a trip in June or July, you will be better off to spend your time in South Dakota. If it's big walleyes you're after, August through October are the prime months for fishing in North Dakota's Lake Sakakawea. The best action is often found in the Van Hook region of the lake near New Town. Here anglers often catch limits of fish averaging OVER six pounds!!

The almost constant winds of the Dakotas can make fishing on some of the bigger expanses of water very dangerous. Anglers are reminded to think of safety FIRST and walleye second.

Access to the river is difficult in some areas. It is not uncommon to travel 50 miles between access points.

166

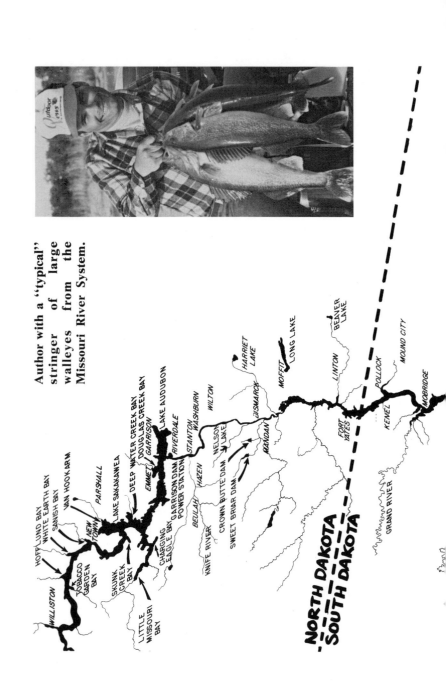

Author with a "typical" stringer of large walleyes from the Missouri River System.

167

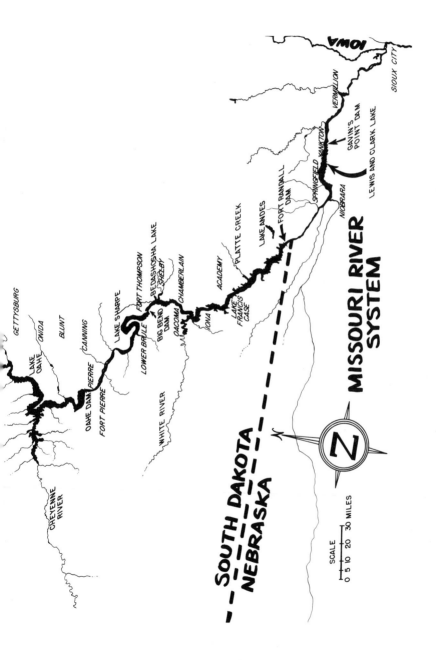

MISSOURI RIVER SYSTEM

Towns, marinas and resorts are also few and far between. Even if you do plan on fishing near a major city, there is a very good chance you will never see another building all day once you leave the dock.

The federal government owns all the land on each side of the river system and if you would like a detailed map showing access points and Corps campground sites contact:

U.S. Army Engineer District - Omaha
6014 U.S. Post Office and Court House
Omaha, Nebraska 68102

LAKE ERIE

In 1970, a ban was placed on the commercial netting of walleyes in Lake Erie. This ban is considered

Signs like this can be found all around the Lake Erie shoreline. This is part of a campaign to tell people that Erie is again worth fishing, and it sure is!

primarily responsible for the sudden explosion in the walleye population. By 1981, many claimed Lake Erie as the walleye capital of the world!

Lake Erie is basically divided into three different basins (see diagram). These different kinds of water and this change in water also limits the range of the walleyes to what they call the Western Basin. This portion of the lake is very shallow, averaging about 26 feet and is

ideal walleye habitat.

In every sense of the word, this lake is a drifter's

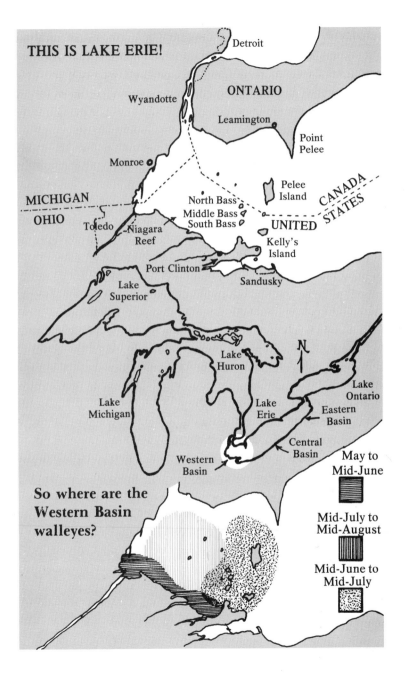

THIS IS LAKE ERIE!

Detroit

ONTARIO

Wyandotte

Leamington

Point Pelee

Monroe

MICHIGAN

OHIO

Toledo

Niagara Reef

Pelee Island

CANADA STATES

North Bass
Middle Bass
South Bass

UNITED

Kelly's Island

Port Clinton

Sandusky

Lake Superior

N

Lake Huron

Lake Ontario

Lake Michigan

Lake Erie

Eastern Basin

Central Basin

Western Basin

May to Mid-June

So where are the Western Basin walleyes?

Mid-July to Mid-August

Mid-June to Mid-July

paradise. The gradual bars and rock areas can extend for miles. Some days, if the wind is right, you could get out to an area and drift all day and never need to start your motor, because schools of walleye just seem to go on and on!

One very interesting thing to note about this particular body of water is that the walleyes often suspend. The reasons for this relates back to their need for food. If they can't find what they need near the bottom, they will surely leave it to find food well above the bottom. This search for food is also responsible for their roaming great distances from shore.

The obvious shifts from one part of the lake to others are predictable. In the spring

Charter boats drift along as anglers catch walleye after walleye.

the walleyes can be found along shore often one to three miles out. By June you can expect to be out seven miles to catch walleyes, and by August you'll often need to travel all the way out to the U.S./Canadian border to find the really big numbers of walleyes.

In my travels to this body of water, finding out where the walleyes were was never a problem, because all you needed to do was follow the other boats! This may sound like cheating but day in and day out this has proven to be the best way to stay with these moving walleyes.

Since the walleyes here suspend off the bottom so often, anglers have developed special techniques to catch them. Drifting methods are used by 90% of the anglers. That is why a good understanding of what happens as your boat drifts over the walleyes is important.

Keeping your bait in front of more unspooked walleyes is the name of the game, so it's to your advantage to cast ahead of the drifting boat or off to the sides. The #1 technique is the "countdown system" using a lure type called a weight-forward spinner. Each manufacturer claims to make the best weight-forward spinner, but personally I never saw much of a difference in the success of one type over another.

Adding a nightcrawler

A typical Erie walleye taken while it was suspended only five feet below the surface!

to your spinner will give you "THE" #1 bait. All you need to do is gob the crawler on the large #2/0 hook so it won't fall off when casting.

The casting of these weight-forward spinners is the best way to catch a quick limit, but if you have a good wind, you might just want to drag it behind the boat using the long lining method. It is interesting to note that although other methods

The West Sister Twister made by the Jen Em Corp. is a popular weight forward spinner. Take special note of how the nightcrawler is threaded on the large hook.

172

of live bait fishing described earlier in this book can be productive, nearly everyone here uses a weight-forward spinner of some sort with a gob of nightcrawler added.

A suspended walleye may be found right below the surface or down twenty feet below it. Each school will often be found at different depths.

The Erie Dearie, a very popular weight-forward spinner rig, is simply deadly on the walleyes found in the Western Basin of Lake Erie.

While drifting, your casts should be made in front of the boat and as the bait hits the water, begin to count. It is a good idea to have other members of the fishing party do this as well. Say it takes 20 seconds for the bait to hit bottom if you were in 25 feet of water. If you wanted the bait to be fished only 12 feet down, you would simply count to ten before you begin your retrieve. Every cast should be a different count until a fish is taken. Then the information should be shared with other members of the boat until fish can no longer be taken. Then everyone should go back to checking different depths.

The time of day for your best success varies with the seasons. On the average, most anglers have their success in the mornings before ten a.m. and again after six p.m.

Although the walleyes here are abundant, Lake Erie is what I would call a quantity lake and not a quality one. The area near Port Clinton is considered the heart of the Western Basin's walleye action with most of the walleyes running two to three pounds. You will rarely see fish in excess of six pounds. In my opinion, the action often makes up for the lack of trophy size

walleyes.

Is Lake Erie an easy place to fish? As long as you treat the lake like an ocean and think safety first, I believe most people can have a real good time catching walleyes.

Charter boat fishermen sort out their morning's catch. Erie walleyes run a consistent two to three pounds with a lot of perch being taken as well.

CANADIAN WALLEYES

Every year thousands of anglers plan their summer vacations to go fishing on a wilderness Canadian lake with visions of catching large golden walleye.

This isn't all bad, in fact, for many years I spent my summers exploring the virgin lakes and rivers of northern Minnesota in the B.W.C.A. (Boundary Waters Canoe Area) and the southern portions of Canada. Back then, catching walleyes was often done out of necessity as a major portion of our meals for long trips. A system soon was put together for catching walleyes quickly and effectively.

Before you settle on a lake for your vacation, it may be to your advantage to find out if the lake has a history of being a quality lake or a quantity one. Lake Kabetogama, for example, is a large shallow lake near the Minnesota-Canadian border. Lake Kabetogama has a great population of two to three pound walleyes. Anglers looking for fast action and lots of fillets for the

174

Not trophies, but some mighty fine eating. These walleyes were taken from a Canadian lake which is known for quantity, not quality.

freezer can't go wrong by fishing here. However, Lake Saganaga (about 100 miles east as the crow flies) is known for its trophy walleyes. The Minnesota state record came from these waters in 1979 and weighed 17½ pounds! Although you may not catch many, the walleyes you do catch may be for the wall instead of the frying pan!

Many of us would give a week's pay to land a twelve pound walleye. Traveling to a trophy fishing lake doesn't always mean you'll catch a trophy walleye. You could spend a whole week of hard fishing without catching a single fish. Very seldom do you find a Canadian wilderness type lake with both quality and quantity.

Due to the colder climate, walleyes found in these northern lakes grow very slowly. A three pound fish might easily be eight years old!

If there were one thing that could help you catch more walleyes from these lakes, it would be wise to remember that the bottom is where you will be finding 90% of your fish. This is vastly different from Lake Erie walleyes where you can expect to catch 80% of the fish five feet above the bottom or more. Your best rigs are ones that can be kept tight to the bottom. The cold Canadian lakes often are not over-run with food; in fact, there is a shortage of food in many cases. When this occurs, even smaller walleyes will fall victim to the survival of the larger ones.

In many virgin Canadian wilderness lakes where the walleyes are hungry, they can be caught on nearly anything! Jigs, for example, will not need the addition of live bait, and the old fashioned plugs like the Rapala and Lazy Ike are deadly!

For the most consistent success at finding walleyes, simply look for rivers flowing into the lake nearest you. The faster the water is pouring into the lake, the better it can be for holding walleye.

A river flowing into a lake as shown here is an ideal spot to find walleyes in a Canadian-type lake all year long!

To be completely honest, this method of looking for the moving water will put you on walleyes 80% of the time! This is a statement that cannot be made about the other methods for finding walleyes in different types of water. The really great thing about this pattern is that you can find walleyes around river mouths all season long! Some days they will be hiding behind rocks in the middle of a raging current and other days they will be holding in the deeper pools near fast water.

Other popular locations for Canadian walleyes would have to include isolated reefs and islands and the narrow but deep channel between the shore and an island. Sand areas are often hard to find in lakes lined with steep rocky banks. Fishing outside a sandy shoreline area can be very productive.

The use of depth finding units in these waters can really help you stay on walleyes, but more times than not when anglers travel to these remote lakes a depth finder is a luxury. That is why a pair of polarized sunglasses can be a new type of "fish finder." These sunglasses do a lot more than just darken a bright day— they greatly help reduce the blinding glare from the water. This will enable you to see things below the surface that might help you find what I call "visual hotspots." These are places that simply look "fishy." While trolling a shoreline you might notice a huge boulder out in the middle of nowhere that you may want to stop and cast to. In rivers you might actually see the white tips on the walleye's tail as the walleye tries to hide behind the rock in shallow water.

In Canadian lakes you very seldom need to fish deeper than 15 feet. One nice thing about the bottom hugging habit these walleyes often have is that you boat doesn't scare the walleyes as often. They feel very secure in their rocks and a motor overhead doesn't seem to bother them.

"If you find one walleye, you've found a school." This statement has never been more true about smaller 1 to 4 pound walleyes from Canadian wilderness type lakes. I've known anglers who would drop anchor in the same spot for three days and not stop catching walleyes! A truly lunker size walleye is more likely to be a loner. It could be their food needs that make them scatter or maybe a territorial habit that walleyes develop. What this often means is that one big walleye doesn't mean you've found the mother lode.

One big problem with fishing these wilderness type lakes found along a major highway is that the walleyes population is often wiped out by angling pressure. Actually, this problem is more widespread than most resort owners would care to admit. The schooling habits of these walleyes leave them easy prey for an experienced angler. Once the school has been reduced from, say, 200 to 25, the odds of your finding those 25 fish are not very good. Cold, infertile lakes found in this northern region just can't replace those fish in a single season; it often takes a dozen years or more for a lake to rebound from heavy fishing pressure.

To get to the best waters today, it is often necessary to portage to a nearby lake which has not received this heavy pressure.

One final thing you may want to be aware of is the razor sharp teeth of the northern pike. This shark of the north country will attack almost anything that moves, especially jigs. Ideally, anglers should tie jigs directly to all their lures to get the best action out of them, but if you run into an area where you keep getting your line broken every time you set the hooks, it's time to use a small wire leader to protect your lures from being lost.

WALLEYES IN WEEDS

When you stop and think about it, a walleye living in the weeds is really not at all surprising. With the range of the walleye expanding to all regions of the country, the walleye still must have the basics of FOOD, SECURITY and COMFORT if they are to live.

A very old lake might be victim to a winter kill every dozen years or so and it never had supported a natural supply of walleyes before. Suddenly the DNR or the locals decide to stock walleyes in the lake. These types of old lakes often do not have much in the way of typical walleye water. The walleyes adapt to the new environment in order to survive. Fishermen serious about catching these weed walleyes must learn to change their thinking as well.

Weed walleyes are not found in large schools. They prefer looser groups of a dozen fish at most. These

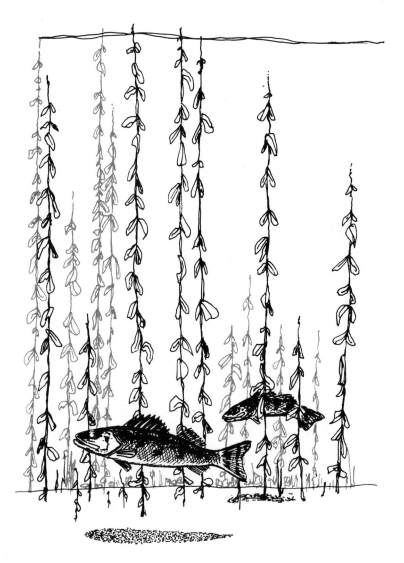

Walleye on the prowl cruise the weeds in loose groups. These walleyes are often taken by bass fishermen by accident.

walleyes will spread out in a given area of weeds and stay there most of the time. It is wise to keep moving and not to spend too long a period fishing any one spot.

In the jumble of weeds found below the surface, the odds of getting your bait in front of a lot of walleyes

A cold front affects weed walleyes by simply pushing the walleyes deep into thick weeds which make them impossible to get a bait to.

spread out in a large area are very slim! They are rarely found in tight schools. Success at catching weed walleyes begins with moving frequently to look for the "easy" fish. Whenever a walleye is in the mood to feed, he often will prowl the tops of the weeds where food is easily spotted. No matter what time of day, you can often expect some walleyes to be cruising the weeds in search of food. If a cold front shuts fishing success down, weed walleyes don't need to leave the weeds, they simply sink deeper into the jungle of weeds tight to the bottom.

Two popular jigs for fishing walleyes in the weeds: the Lund Backswimmer (left) and the Mister Twister swirl tails.

Weed walleyes are often found in very shallow water, which is why artificial lures can be used with excellent results. Rapalas and many of the bass fisherman's chunky looking crankbaits are fantastic. Grub bodies on jigs like the Lund Backswimmer or Mister Twister swirl tail jigs are very effective too. One-eighth ounce jigs are often your best bet to keep the jig from sinking too quickly in the weeds.

Some lakes may have deep weeds growing down to twenty feet, while in other lakes the weed growth ends at only five feet. It makes little difference what depth or type of weed a lake may have, just as long as it's thick enough for a walleye to hide.

Although it is best to "keep moving," you want to be sure you thoroughly saturate the weed beds as you move along. Again polarized sunglasses can be a big in spotting the openings in the weeds below the surface.

Bobber fishing is also effective for fishing in weeds. The only problem with this method is that the weeds are often full of bait-snatching panfish and perch. This is the major reason artificial lures can be more practical in weeds.

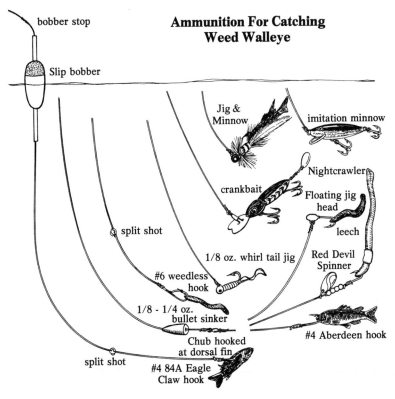

Ammunition For Catching Weed Walleye

bobber stop

Slip bobber

Jig & Minnow

imitation minnow

crankbait

Nightcrawler

Floating jig head

leech

split shot

1/8 oz. whirl tail jig

Red Devil Spinner

#6 weedless hook

1/8 - 1/4 oz. bullet sinker

#4 Aberdeen hook

Chub hooked at dorsal fin

split shot

#4 84A Eagle Claw hook

Here is a selection of various lures and live bait rigs that can be used for weed walleye.

Locating which weed areas are holding walleye often starts by finding the deepest and thickest weed beds available in a particular lake. This can usually be done simply by driving your boat around the lake and looking into the water. If the areas all seem to look the same then fish the weedy points or sunken islands first.

These form some common irregularities that might hold a larger group of walleyes. Many times the best producing pockets or small points are only found by spending the time to fish an area first.

Fishing walleyes in the weeds can add a whole new dimension to your fishing. It is definitely the most difficult of all areas to fish with consistent success.

FISHING A NEW LAKE

Probably the most enjoyable thing about my job is that I travel to all regions of the country meeting new people and fishing new lakes. During most years, I can expect to launch my boat on at least fifty new lakes. So far this book has shown you many different aspects of walleye fishing techniques. Knowing when to apply a particular method for the best results is a combination of experience and confidence.

You may be fishing on a lake where the local people can't catch a walleye, but using a standard live bait rig and backtrolling along a sunken island you catch six nice fish. Using a little fishing logic and a blend of practical experience you can catch fish on ANY lake.

Every region of the country seems to have its own special trick for catching walleyes. In this book it would be impossible to talk about them all. The basic bread and butter methods I have chosen to describe have NEVER proven to be completely out of place. That is why if you're out on a new lake, it is important you fish YOUR way first. If, for some reason, you cannot find or catch fish, it's time to find out how the locals do it.

I can remember one lake in Wisconsin where the locals had never seen a walleye over four pounds come from their lake, but when I started fishing on the first obvious point, not more than one hundred yards from the boat ramp, the walleye had a different story.

Using the standard method of casting a light jig to

Here is a nice limit of walleyes taken by the author (left) and Paul Sokol from a lake in Wisconsin that locals just don't fish for walleyes.

shallow water, I took an easy limit of fish within a half hour and six out of the ten were OVER four pounds! I was in the right place at the right time for sure, but the message here is to stick to the basics, and the methods you know best!

Before heading into a new area, some research work is necessary. By taking the time to learn helpful background information, you will be in a better position to decide which lakes are worth fishing first. Contact the Department of Natural Resources for any information on lakes you may want to fish. They keep on file all the stocking programs for each lake and records of test nettings to give you some idea of how abundant the walleye population is.

With some additional checking at local bait shops you can often find out which lakes have been producing. Weekly fishing entries often reflect which lakes have been doing well.

When it comes right down to it, being on the "hot" lake will save time and effort. Some guides freely give valuable information, such as the depth of water the fish are coming from, the kind of bottom they are preferring, baits, the time of day for best success; then the same guy will clam up when you stick a map in front of his face and ask him to mark all of his spots.

The key to zeroing in on a particular lake is getting to talk to people who have actually taken walleyes from the lake recently. Second and third hand information often isn't complete enough to help in many cases.

The cardinal sin in asking a question of someone who knows where the walleyes are biting is the blunt statement, "Where did you catch 'em?"

When the local guide stops by the local bait shop to show off his huge stringer of walleyes, this is a prime opportunity for you to get the information you need. Remember, never ask WHERE they were caught, instead ask questions like time of day for best success, the best baits or rigs that he had success with, was he trolling or anchored? Are the fish still being caught? How

how deep of water were they in?

In your questioning, be sure you are asking in a friendly way as not to seem like you're badgering the guide. By this time you might get a chance to look in his boat and study the way he is rigged to fish, i.e. what color lures, what size sinkers, the length of snell if using a live bait rig, and take note of any special gimmicks he may have in the boat. These are all things that can help you save time and effort in your search for walleyes.

LAKE MAPS A lake map serves as a great time saving tool. The general information it can supply about bottom contours can give you some great places to start fishing.

Bringing along a grease pencil or pen to mark your best spots is an important tip that can play off big in years to come. You never know when you may want to come back to this newly discovered lake and your memory might not recall all the possible "hotspots."

Marking a map as you fish gives you helpful information to help others or if you plan or returning to the lake in a few years.

At home you can examine a lake map and circle areas that appear most promising. It is very easy to get distracted while fishing and not get to fish as much of the lake as possible. The real key to success in fishing a new lake is to try fishing many different parts of the lake that look similar to places you have fished before.

Once you have fished all these likely spots and you can't seem to find any walleyes, there are two things you can do.

1.   Select the area you believe to have the highest potential for holding walleyes. Refish the area using every trick on presentation talked about in this book. Sometimes you will need to bear down on a particular area and just fish it hard.

2.   Load your boat and head to another lake! No matter how many fishing decals you have on your boat, if the fish don't want to bite, they won't!

Having confidence is an important factor when fishing a new lake. That is why you shouldn't frustrate yourself with a tough fishing lake for very long. Many times you will have no control over the outcome of the day. You can only do your best.

When fishing a very large lake, the WORST possible thing you can do is go for a boat ride all day. Instead, concentrate on one section of the lake at a time. It is very easy to get caught up in the old cliche' "the fish always bite better on the other side of the lake."

If you put together a game plan of attack when fishing with two or more boats you can really save time. Very simply, it just takes a lot of man hours to find the good fishing areas. If three boats are all looking in different areas and fishing different ways it often doesn't take long for someone to start

Working as a team in three separate boats, these happy anglers zeroed in on the walleyes and it payed off big!

catching fish. If you can plan the group to get together

every few hours to compare notes, your efforts will benefit all. This kind of team work fishing is great fun and an excellent way to learn a new lake.

188

Trouble Shooting Tips

CATCHING SUSPENDED WALLEYE In the section on fishing Lake Erie for walleyes, we found they suspend a great deal of the time. The count down method of fishing with weight forward spinners is used here almost exclusively. Many times I have tried this method of fishing on other lakes with only limited success. There are several different ways to present your bait to suspended fish.

Finding walleyes that suspend is common during mid-summer on lakes that are large and shallow. A walleye will suspend for many different reasons, but their need for finding food is probably the most logical explanation. Without the use of a graph-type sonar unit, it would be nearly impossible to zero in on the depth that is holding walleyes. Finding suspended fish is really what the graph units do best. Of course, you will never know for sure what you are finding on the chart units until you

A graph unit excels in areas where walleyes are prone to suspend.

actually catch a fish, but at least you will have a much better idea of what depth to start fishing.

Trying to catch suspended walleyes with any consistency at all is one of the most difficult things to do. This is why I often tell anglers not to worry about fishing for suspended fish.

When you do find walleyes suspending four feet or less above the bottom, it is often best to use one of the many floating rigs. Anglers must be aware of the speed they are fishing in order for the floating rigs to rise off bottom. Water resistance can easily pull the bait back toward the bottom. The name of the game when fishing a floating rig is to move VERY slowly. (See diagram.)

SUSPENDED WALLEYE TRICKS

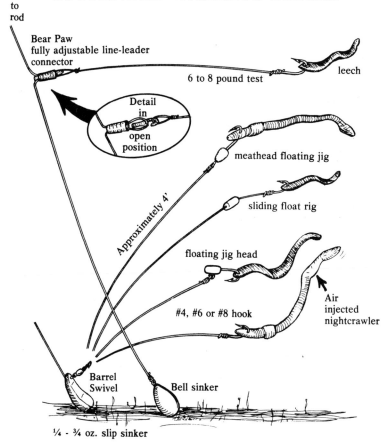

to rod

Bear Paw
fully adjustable line-leader
connector

6 to 8 pound test

leech

Detail in open position

meathead floating jig

sliding float rig

Approximately 4'

floating jig head

Air injected nightcrawler

#4, #6 or #8 hook

Barrel Swivel

Bell sinker

¼ - ¾ oz. slip sinker

When you find walleyes suspending five feet of more above the bottom, it becomes very difficult to control your distance above the bottom with a floating rig. Now you will be better off using a dropper rig. This rig resembles the Wolf River Rig, except the line from the three-way swivel is much longer. Instead of a swivel, you can use a Bear Paw connector. The snell should be four feet ong with a spinner or floating jig head to keep the hook as straight behind the swivel or connector as possible. With this method you can drift or troll much more quickly than with the rigs that need to be floated up from the bottom. The secret to making this rig really perform is using a very heavy sinker to keep it dragging the bottom.

Sliding bobber rigs are also effective on suspended fish. Walleyes often suspend near a reef or bar. A walleye in summer will often follow the baitfish into deep water without any concern for the bottom. When the baitfish return to the reefs in the morning and evening hours the walleyes come back to the areas along the bottom where most anglers catch them. All during the day, suspended walleyes might be only fifty yards away, suspended in deep water. You could be into action all day long if you were able to predict how they would move in and out. These walleyes can often be caught by using a sliding bobber rig and simply dangling a juicy morsel right in front of their noses. They will often suspend at the same depth anglers most often catch them at when they move to the reefs.

If, for example, one morning you catch six nice fish from twelve feet of water tight to the bottom along a steep drop-off and suddenly your success stops, the walleyes might still be in twelve feet of water, but are now suspended thirty yards away over thirty feet of water! Drifting outward from previously productive areas with a slip bobber rig will help you find those walleyes again. Don't count on dropping an anchor and catching a limit either. These walleyes are not only extremely spooky, but also move around a lot to follow the food.

NIGHT FISHING Many of us would like to catch more and bigger walleyes this season. So far all the tips and methods in the book will help in some way or another to put more fish in the boat, or at least give you a very good idea of why you aren't catching them. One major factor in your walleye fishing success lies with your being on the lake when the walleyes want to feed. This time is often during the night!

One of the well known facts about walleyes is that night fishing can be very productive. Many anglers have been bold enough to give night fishing a try, but often lose interest quickly in the isolation of the night. Finding shortcuts to better night fishing will begin long BEFORE the lights go out! Good

Big walleye at night are on the prowl to feed. To the angler willing to put out the extra effort, big fish like this will be your reward.

planning is of prime importance to productive walleye fishing at night. This planning begins with a good look at the lake and what it has to offer.

Night time walleyes often feed on windswept points or reefs in only a few feet of water. One of the biggest problems you'll have at night is knowing if you are fishing the right spot. By taking the time during the DAY to lcoate possible hotspots and marking them with inexpensive buoys, you will be able to return to the area at night and fish more productively.

Techniques for fooling those walleyes will vary a lot from lake to lake depending mostly on bottom content. In an extremely rocky area where snags will be a constant problem, a sliding bobber rig will work just great. Sometimes you will find walleyes scattered along a shoreline at night in only inches of water. A lead headed jig is a great way to cover lots of water in a very tempting way for a walleye. ⅛ and ¼ ounce jigs are the best sizes over all. The more snags you run into, the lighter the jig you should use. The best shaped jig head for this purpose is the stand-up or wedge-shaped head. While casting and dragging the jig along the bottom, these jig heads will keep the hook pointed upwards when you don't move it. A round headed jig rolls on its side and can get snagged much easier, but worse yet, the walleyes can't get hold of the hook as easily.

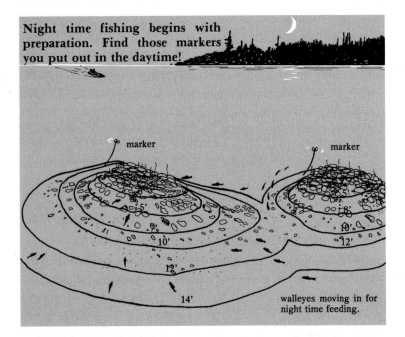

Night time fishing begins with preparation. Find those markers you put out in the daytime!

marker

marker

5'

10'

12'

14'

8'

10'

12'

walleyes moving in for night time feeding.

Casting or trolling plugs like the Rapala or Lazy Ike can be one of the best ways to catch walleyes at night. These night walleyes are often too shallow to do only one thing—EAT! A walleye will attack an artificial lure so hard, you might think you're fighting a bass or northern pike.

These three methods for catching walleyes are nothing new, but using them at night when you range of sight ends at your

Shore fishing near river mouths, boat channels and swimming beaches at night has its rewards.

rod tip is another matter. To be truly productive at night, an angler must first get very familiar with how his equipment works during the daylight hours. Many anglers prefer to use the spincast or push button type of reel at night because they are nearly tangle-free. It may seem silly and a waste of time to practice casting the lures you will use, but knowing how your baits are working will save you a lot of wasted time.

Be sure your boat is equipped with Coast Guard approved lights. Bobber fishermen often suspend a lantern from a long pole above the boat. If you are casting or trolling you must keep at least one white light on so others can see you. This is often just enough light to see what you're doing as well. It sometimes helps to keep a small dim light in the boat so you can quickly use it for tying knots and such. You do not want to be constantly turning lights on and off because you will lose your night vision. A hand held spotlight should be used to help you find your way back to the dock. If you are out by yourself, it may be a good idea to

194

tape an inexpensive flashlight to the handle of your net so you will be able to see the walleyes better when you do need to land one.

Bugs can often be a problem at sundown and they are one of the major reasons most folks don't do much night fishing in the summer months. A few hours after sundown, however, many of the bugs have left for the evening.

Night fishing is a sport that begins long before the sun goes down. The shy and lazy daytime walleye turns into an aggressive beast by night. There is no doubt about the fact that night time IS walleye time. Sure it's more work, and sure it may not be as fun as fishing during the day, but it sure can put some nice walleyes in the boat.

THE IMPORTANCE OF CLEAN HANDS Can fish smell? You bet! It's no secret, no miracle breakthrough, but if you are interested in catching more fish this summer, you can start by simply cleaning your hands regularly. It's a good habit to get into. Having clean hands is one of the basic rules among veteran anglers. Outboard motor gas, suntan lotion, reel oil and insect repellent are used nearly everytime we go fishing, and can turn aggressive fish off like a switch.

A regular bar of soap will do just fine. Biodegradable soaps are highly recommended. Anglers can store a bottle or bar of soap in the back splashwell of their boat for easy access. The squeeze bottles of dishwater soaps are very convenient and easy to buy, and you don't have to worry about dropping or storing these containers of soap.

A clean, dry towel should be kept in the boat to dry your hands between fish . . . a lot better than wiping them on dirty jeans. Wipe all of your equipment clean of excess grease and oil. Your steering wheel or control handle should be kept clean as well. Wipe all excess oil from your reels after they have been lubricated.

A gassy smell on your line or sinkers will do more to ruin your fishing than a cold front! It is very important to store your equipment in a clean, dry place.

Anise oil has long been used as an attractor by old timers. This oil smells a lot like licorice. Now I don't know if fish like the smell of licorice, but this type of smell doesn't seem to hurt your ability to catch fish. Many tackle companies make fishing soaps with anise oil added. When this is done, you have a soap that may be doubly good.

In the old days, my grandfather would spit on his hook with a little tobacco snoose. It wasn't until I became aware of the fish's ability to smell that I realized why he did it. Tobacco also can be used to remove any foreign smells from a bait and will not affect the fish's willingness to strike.

SHARP HOOKS The more you get into walleye fishing, the more you realize the importance of the little things that can be the difference between catching twelve fish a day instead of seven or eight.

Having a good sharp hook rates in importance right up there with good knots and a strong hookset.

By simply taking the time to periodically check your hooks for sharpness, you will find your hooksets will penetrate the bony jaw of the walleye much easier.

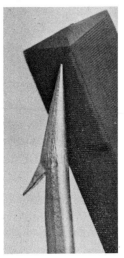

The procedure for sharpening a hook is actually very simple. First, you will need a small knife sharpening stone or jewelers file. Start on the outside of the dulled point, working in only one direction toward the hook's eye. By making several passes with a stone or file, your hook is often needle sharp again and ready for fishing. If your hook gets caught on a rock or log, check it right away. If the tip has been cracked off, then you'd best just throw it away and replace it with another hook.

NETTING A WALLEYE   After you have hooked that trophy walleye of a lifetime, it may be a good idea to know the proper way to handle a landing net. I've found a method which works very well for netting any type of fish.

You must not be overly excited and nervous about the fish and try to net it before it's lying ON THE SURFACE and ready to be netted. You never want to make any deep water attacks at the fish with the net. DO NOT put the net in the water before the fish is ready to be netted. The fish should be

Netting a walleye is a simple task as long as you try not to get too nervous.

skimmed off the surface with one continuous motion from HEAD to TAIL.

Always keep the net in a tangle free position. The last thing you will need while a ten pound walleye is fighting for her life is a Chinese fire drill to untangle the net from the oars or the other rods and reels.

Cloth mesh nets should be replaced regularly to prevent fish from swimming right through the old netting. Rubber nets are something new on the market and fine for bass, but if you plan on landing a lot of walleyes, I advise using a nylon or cloth-type net. I also like to use nets with fairly long handles; it gives me an opportunity to make a bigger sweep in the water. This will help in landing a bigger fish.

A landing net is a very important piece of equipment

that shouldn't be skimped on. Take the time to learn the proper way to use it so when that ten pound walleye does hit, getting him into the boat will be the easy part.

THE IMPORTANCE OF RAINGEAR Many a walleye trip is made when the weather conditions are far from ideal. A little rain or wind should never ruin a trip, and knowing how to select the proper raingear is the key.

It is never a good idea to skimp on the type of raingear you buy. Basically you have four different types of material to choose from: plastics, which are inexpensive; coated fabrics, which are tough; rubber, which is popular among commercial fishermen; and the newest space-age meterial called Gore-tex. This material is expensive, but is capable of breathing, so you won't get as hot when you wear articles made from it.

The price you pay will reflect on the lifespan and actual ability to keep you dry. This is a very good investment to make if you plan on spending a great deal of time out of doors.

TAKING CARE OF YOUR CATCH When you come right down to it, why are so many people into walleye fishing? It sure isn't their spectacular leaps or powerful runs that make them so popular. The real bottom line is that people love to eat walleyes. The best restaurants in the country serve walleye because it is one of the finest eating fish in freshwater.

What really hurts me is the poor way many people take care of the fish they catch. Some complain that the walleyes taste muddy or oily and many times it's their own fault! A walleye is a very valuable resource that we can't afford to waste.

Let's take a look at some of the best ways to insure that the walleyes you catch this season will taste as good as they possibly can.

A fish stringer is a popular way to hold your fish.

198

There is no better way to hold walleye until they are cleaned than to keep them on ice. Whenever possible, bring along a cooler with ice for your walleyes.

Hook the rope or clips through BOTH lips of the walleye to prevent the fish from swallowing too much water as you drag him around. Stay away from clip-type stringers unless they have a special locking feature to prevent the walleye from getting away. As soon as the fish die, DO NOT continue to drag them around because now they will begin to absorb the bad flavors of oil or a "muddy" taste. It is extremely critical that you clean the walleyes or put them on ice as soon as they die if you have any intension of eating them. You simply can't drag around dead fish all day on a stringer and expect them to taste good at dinner.

We have already talked about live wells for walleyes and how in many cases, except for the early spring and fall seasons, water temperatures often kill the walleyes you catch in a very short period of time. Again, live wells are nice, but sometimes they just will not work for the purpose intended. A live well can easily become an ice cooler for keeping your walleyes fresh.

FILLETING YOUR WALLEYE When filleting your walleye, make sure your knife is sharp before you begin. A sharp knife cuts cleaner, easier and with less effort. It takes practice to become quick at filleting walleyes, so don't rush yourself.

HOW TO FILLET WALLEYE

1. First, make a cut down to the bone just behind the gills.
2. Turn the blade on its side while resting on the backbone and start cutting toward the tail. You now have the first half removed. Turn the fish over and repeat the process. Take your time and try to keep the knife as close to the backbone as possible to save every tasty morsel.

3. Lay both fillets skin side down and cut away the stomach lining and the rib bones. The fillet knife should slide just under the rib bones.

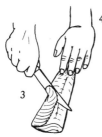

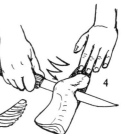

4. Now, with the knife, separate skin from flesh at the tail portion. Hold the skin with thumb and index finger, or pin it to the working surface with your fingernails as you prepare to "see-saw" the blade between the skin and flesh at a 30° downward angle as you pull on the outside skin. You are not finished yet!

5. Getting the cheek meat out is the final step. Actually, it's the fleshy part of the gill covering that should be dug out with the point of the knife. Use a circular cutting motion and then scoop out the meat. Separate the skin from the flesh and repeat the process for the other gill covering and there you have it! Two nice fillets, plus the cheek meat ready for the frying pan or the freezer. A quart milk container can be used to freeze the cheeks until you have enough for a meal. Just add cheeks and water each time you fillet until the container is full. Good eating!

There are many ways known to fillet a fish. The method shown here is the best one we've found. It's quick, easy, and keeps waste to a minimum. It has been around for a long time and will continue to be a popular way to process those delicious walleye.

If you land a very large walleye and find the fillets are thicker than one inch, it may be best to cut the fillets to make them thinner. A thinner fillet cooks up much nicer and will taste better. You can also slice the fillets into thin strips about an inch thick to insure that all the fillets will cook evenly. Everyone says that the smaller fish taste better, why? It's because most people try to fry fillets that are a half-inch thick with fillets that are two inches thick and are disappointed by the mushy or fishy texture of the thick fillets. Big fish DO taste good as long as they are prepared properly.

To freeze walleye fillets, you are best off to put them in any empty milk carton filled with water. Heavy duty freezer bags filled with water can work too, but if you plan on keeping those fillets frozen for more than a few weeks, the use of a milk carton filled with water is the best way to prevent freezer burn or just flat tasting fish.

A great meal of walleye begins as soon as you catch it. A little extra effort on the water will insure a better tasting walleye dinner.

BEER BATTER WALLEYE

3 lbs. walleye fillets
1 cup flour
1 tsp. salt
1 tsp. baking soda
1 can beer
1 egg
peanut oil (shortening)

Wash fillets. Cut into serving size pieces. Stir together dry ingredients. Add beer and egg; stir until consistency is like a thick gravy. Heat peanut oil or shortening (1½ to 2 inches) to 375 degrees in skillet. Fry each side of fillet until golden brown. Drain on paper towel. Season to taste.

CRACKER MEAL WALLEYE

walleye fillets
4 eggs
1½ cups milk
2 cup flour
2 - 2½ cups finely chopped saltine crackers
peanut oil (shortening)

Wash fillets and cut into serving pieces. Stir together eggs and milk. Coat fillet with flour; dip into egg mixture, then coat with cracker crumbs. Heat peanut oil or shortening (1½ to 2 inches) to 375 degrees in skillet. Fry until golden brown on both sides. Drain, Season to taste.

BAKED WALLEYE (WITH WHITE SAUCE)

3-4 lbs. walleye fillets
¼ cup butter
salt
pepper

Heat oven to 400 degrees. If fillets are large, cut into serving size pieces. Place fillets in greased shallow pan. Season with salt and pepper; brush with melted butter. Bake 15-30 minutes.

WHITE SAUCE

2 tbsp. butter
2 tbsp. flour
1 cup milk
½ tsp. salt
⅛ tsp. pepper
2 hard boiled eggs (diced)

Put butter in heavy saucepan, and melt over low heat. Blend in flour, salt and pepper. Cook over low heat until smooth and bubbly. Remove from heat. Stir in milk and bring to boil. Boil for one minute. Add diced eggs and stir. Pour over fillets and serve.

STUFFED WALLEYE

Preheat oven to 375 degrees

2½ - 3 lb. walleye (with scales removed and fish gutted)
4 cups bread crumbs
2 tbsp. chopped onions
½ cup chopped celery
¼ cup melted fat
3 - 4 strips of bacon
hot water
salt
pepper

Mix all ingredients. Add enough hot water to moisten. Gently fill walleye with stuffing. Use toothpicks to close opening. Coat with melted fat. Top with bacon strips. Bake 25 - 30 minutes.

STATE WALLEYE RECORDS

State	Weight	Name	Lake	Year
Alabama	10-4	Julia Hurley	Weis Lake	1980
Arizona	8-1	Bud Clifford	Lake Powell	1977
Arkansas	21-9	E.D. Claibourne	Little Red River	1979
Colorado	16-8	Julius Stever	Cherry Creek Reservoir	1973
Connecticut	14-8	George Britte	Candlewood Lake	1941
Georgia	11-0	Steven Kenny	Lake Borton	1963
Idaho	7-11	William H. Noh	Salmon Falls Reservoir	1981
Illinois	14-0	Fred Goselin	Kankakee River	1961
Indiana	14-4 (tie)	Leon Richart	Kankakee River	1974
		Donald Tedford	Tippecanoe River	1977
Iowa	14-2	Herbert Aldridge	Spirit Lake	1968
Kansas	13-1	David Watson	Rocky Ford	1972
Kentucky	21-8	Abe Black	Lake Cumberland	1958
Maryland	11-0	Thomas J. Broskey	Mill Run	1976
Massachusetts	11-0	no name given	Ovasbin Reservoir	1973
Michigan	17-3	Ray Fadley	Pine River	1951
Minnesota	17-8	LeRoy Chiovitte	Seagull River	1979
Mississippi	8-4	Ruble Bowen	Bull Mountain Creek	1980
Missouri	20-0	John T. Vocholek	St. Francis River	1961
Montana	14-0	Neil Berg	Nelson Reservoir	1974
Nebraska	16-2	Herbert J. Cutshall	Lake McConaughy	1971
Nevada	12-13	David A. Bjorlin	Humbolt River	1981

STATE WALLEYE RECORDS (Continued)

State	Weight	Name	Lake	Year
New Hampshire	11-8	James Bennett, Sr.	Connecticut River	1979
New Jersey	12-13	Stanley Norman	Delaware River	1934
New Mexico	13-0	Jim Scearee	Clayton Lake	1981
New York	15-3	Blanche Baker	Chemung River	1952
North Carolina	13-4	Leonard Williams	Santeetah Reservoir	1966
North Dakota	15-12	B. Chapman	Wood Lake	1959
Ohio	15-1¼	Steve Slawinski	Maumee River	1980
Oklahoma	11-4	Garret Knol	Lake Hefner	1967
Oregon	13-0	Paul Adams	Columbia River	1982
Pennsylvania	17-9	Mike Holly	Kinzua Lake	1980
South Carolina	9-0	Terry O. Sheriff	Lake Hartwell	1974
South Dakota	15-3	George Heyde	Lake Sharpe	1979
Tennesse	25-0	Mabry Harper	Old Hickory Reservoir	1960
Texas	11-15¾	Ray Thrailkill	Lake Meredith	1981
Utah	11-12	Edward Hackanson	Utah Lake	1978
Vermont	12-8	Michael Kebalka	Connecticut River	1981
Virginia	22-8	Roy G. Barret	New River	1973
Washington	16-15	no name given	Roosevelt Lake	1977
West Virginia	16-19	E.C. Cox	New River	1967
Wisconsin	18-0	Tony Brothers	High Lake	1933
Wyoming	14-4	Wilmer Swindler	Keyhold Reservoir	1973

MEET THE AUTHOR

Tom Zenanko hails from Minneapolis and is a full-time outdoor writer/photographer who appears in many national, regional and local publications. As one of the country's leading authorities on freshwater fishing, Tom gives over one hundred fishing seminars annually and also serves as a fishing consultant for many of the country's largest fishing tackle companies. Tom has spent the better part of his life traveling the country in search of walleyes and freely shares his experiences with anglers of all ages.